HIDDEN TREASURES
OF ANCIENT EGYPT

Unearthing the Masterpieces of Egyptian History

ZAHI HAWASS

PHOTOGRAPHS BY KENNETH GARRETT

NATIONAL GEOGRAPHIC

WASHINGTON, D.C.

CONTENTS

STATUE OF A SCRIBE
Painted Limestone
Height 51 cm
Saqqara
Dynasty 5

THE EGYPTIAN MUSEUM, CAIRO

STATUE OF STANDING MAN
Painted limestone
Height 59 cm
Old Kingdom
Giza
Abu Bakr excavation, circa 1950

THE ARTIFACTS AT THE CAIRO MUSEUM REPRESENT THE best that ancient Egypt has to offer. There are fabulous statues, incredible jewels of glittering gold and precious stones, miles of inscribed and decorated reliefs, the coffins and sarcophagi and mummies of kings, pottery spanning the ages, and countless pieces classified as minor but that are far from unimportant. Exploring the museum properly takes weeks—it is a vast storehouse of aesthetic pleasures and scholarly satisfaction.

The museum itself is an international treasure. It was opened in November 1902 and was planned from the outset as a place to store and exhibit artifacts. Its collections are unparalleled, and it is visited by thousands of tourists each day. The year 2002 marked the 100th birthday of the museum. I had just taken on the job of secretary general of the Supreme Council of Antiquities (SCA), and it was my great honor and pleasure to help oversee the festivities. It was a wonderful event, with fireworks and a laser show with photos illustrating the history of the museum. Mrs. Suzanne Mubarak, wife of Egypt's president, Hosni Mubarak, and Farouk Hosni, Minister of Culture, gave speeches, and scholars from all over the world came to talk about the museum's collections. Everyone dressed in period clothes, and music from a hundred years ago was played. The entire western courtyard of the museum was cleaned and renovated, and a huge tent was erected to house the celebration.

As part of these festivities, we brought together 250 objects that were either lying neglected in the basement of the museum, a maze of mysterious corridors filled with boxes of artifacts; hidden in plain sight—on display at the museum but overlooked by most tourists; or stored in magazines scattered around Egypt, where they had been seen by no one but their excavators. Everyone was amazed that we were able to pull these pieces together, especially since we only had a few weeks to do so. I nicknamed the project Mission Impossible. I was on my cell phone constantly, helping with logistical problems, keeping in touch with worried committee members, encouraging the movers and inspectors, and reassuring foreign archaeologists who were worried about the safety of their finds. But we discovered wonderful objects at the museum, and brought many others to Cairo from sites around Egypt. A number of these are now displayed in special galleries in the basement of the museum as a new exhibit, "Hidden Treasures of the Egyptian Museum."

The centennial exhibit represents a new and critical landmark in the history of the museum. Beginning what will be an ongoing reexploration and recataloguing of the basement storerooms is an important step in the modernization of the museum itself. We are ushering in a new era of museum display, with informative labels and modern, uncluttered presentations.

At the opening of this exhibit, we honored the past directors of the Cairo Museum and took a look back at the history of archaeology in Egypt, paying homage to great men such as Ahmed Pasha Kamal (the first native Egyptologist) and Hag Ahmed Youssef (our greatest conservator, the man who restored the boat of Khufu at Giza). We presented the giants of the past with a statue of Ma'at, goddess of justice and truth, and the National Geographic showed a half-hour film about the exhibit.

Carefully chosen objects from the Hidden Treasures exhibit form the core of this book. Complementing them are other, better-known pieces from the permanent collection of the museum. Working with these objects has opened my eyes to the tales that artifacts have to tell, from stories about the men and women who made and used them, to the adventures of the archaeologists who dedicated their lives to finding them—men and women full of passion for the past. Woven into the stories of these beautiful objects is the history of Egyptian archaeology over the last century and a half, from the founding of the Antiquities Service and the first attempts to keep Egypt's heritage within its borders, to the present. This is a fascinating tale, set against a backdrop of the slow decline of colonialism and the struggle of modern Egyptians to reclaim pride and control of their own ancient heritage.

The book is divided into three parts. The first covers the period from 1850 to 1950, and focuses on artifacts found during the first century of the Egyptian Antiquities Service, now the Supreme Council of Antiquities. Through these priceless objects, we will meet some of the giants of the early years, including Egyptian scholars whose contributions were neglected by the foreigners who then dominated the field.

The second part of the book tells the story of the more recent past, from the 1950s, when the Egyptian Antiquities Service was finally placed in Egyptian hands, to the present. As we travel through the past five decades, I will take you to visit some of my own excavations, and share with you some of the fabulous objects I have found over the course of the three decades of my own career. The last section is dedicated to excavations that I have initiated recently and that are ongoing, giving the reader a glimpse into the latest great discoveries in Egypt. These discoveries have not been made at Giza, the site of the majority of my work and my favorite place in Egypt, but at other sites in Upper Egypt. The missions at these sites are all staffed completely by Egyptians.

I am aided in my work by a number of well-trained Egyptian archaeologists. I depend on my close assistants and associates: Mahmoud Afifi and Mansour Boriak, who supervise my work at Giza; Tarek el-Awady, who has participated in excavations in the Bahariya Oasis; archaeologists Ramadan Badr, Hussein Abdou el-Basir, Mohamed Ismail, Mohamed Megahed, and Abdel-Hakeim Karara; epigraphers Noha Abdel Hafiz and and Amani Abdel Hamied, and my irreplaceable assistant Nashwa Gaber. These young men and women are bright and energetic, and promise a brilliant future for Egyptian archaeology.

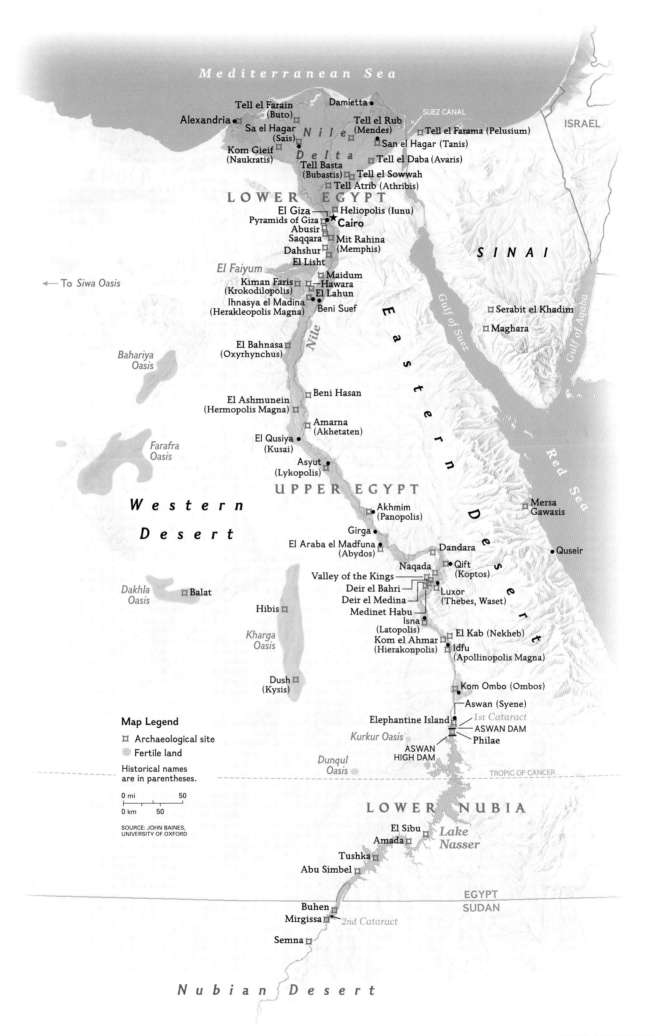

Mediterranean Sea

ISRAEL

SUEZ CANAL

Tell el Farain
(Buto)
Damietta •
Alexandria •
Sa el Hagar
(Sais)
Tell el Rub
(Mendes)
Tell el Farama (Pelusium)
San el Hagar (Tanis)
Kom Gieif
(Naukratis)
Nile
Delta
Tell el Daba (Avaris)
Tell Basta
(Bubastis)
Tell el Sowwah
Tell Atrib (Athribis)

LOWER EGYPT

El Giza
Heliopolis (Iunu)
Pyramids of Giza
★ Cairo
Abusir
Saqqara
Mit Rahina
Dahshur
(Memphis)
El Lisht

El Faiyum

← To *Siwa Oasis*

Maidum
Kiman Faris
(Krokodilopolis)
Hawara
El Lahun
Ihnasya el Madina
(Herakleopolis Magna)
Beni Suef

SINAI

Gulf of Suez

Serabit el Khadim

Maghara

Gulf of Aqaba

*Bahariya
Oasis*

El Bahnasa
(Oxyrhynchus)

Nile

*E
a
s
t
e
r
n*

Beni Hasan

El Ashmunein
(Hermopolis Magna)

Red Sea

*Farafra
Oasis*

Amarna
(Akhetaten)
El Qusiya
(Kusai)

Asyut
(Lykopolis)

UPPER EGYPT

*Western
Desert*

Akhmim
(Panopolis)

Mersa
Gawasis

Girga •

El Araba el Madfuna
(Abydos)

Dandara

*D
e
s
e
r
t*

• Quseir

*Dakhla
Oasis*
Balat

Hibis

Naqada
Qift
(Koptos)
Valley of the Kings
Deir el Bahri
Deir el Medina
Luxor
(Thebes, Waset)
Medinet Habu
Isna
(Latopolis)
El Kab (Nekheb)
Kom el Ahmar
(Hierakonpolis)
Idfu
(Apollinopolis Magna)

*Kharga
Oasis*

Dush
(Kysis)

Kom Ombo (Ombos)

Aswan (Syene)

Map Legend

⊡ Archaeological site
▨ Fertile land
Historical names
are in parentheses.

0 mi   50
0 km   50

SOURCE: JOHN BAINES,
UNIVERSITY OF OXFORD

Elephantine Island
Kurkur Oasis
1st Cataract
ASWAN DAM
Philae
ASWAN
HIGH DAM

*Dunqul
Oasis*

TROPIC OF CANCER

LOWER NUBIA

El Sibu
Amada
*Lake
Nasser*
Tushka
Abu Simbel

EGYPT
SUDAN

Buhen
Mirgissa
2nd Cataract

Semna

Nubian Desert

We are now entering a new era in Egyptian archaeology. There is a new spirit of cooperation between Egyptian and foreign archaeologists (although the sailing is not always smooth), and a new awareness of our joint responsibility for the great monuments of Egypt. I am privileged to know and work with many great scholars, both Egyptian and foreign, for the preservation of Egypt's heritage, and count archaeologists from America, Germany, the Czech Republic, England, and Poland among my closest friends and most dependable colleagues.

For several decades, I have been in charge of the pyramid fields at Giza and Saqqara, and since April 2002, I have served as secretary general of the Supreme Council of Antiquities. I am honored to be entrusted with our shared cultural heritage. Over the course of my career, I have created and taken the first steps toward executing site management plans designed to protect the sites under my care, to combat the dangers that threaten our monuments. These include visitor centers, sidewalks to keep tourists from touching the monuments, new labs, and work plans focused on conservation and restoration. Many of my own discoveries were made as a result of a focus on the preservation and protection of the ancient monuments. I am now concentrating on creating new rules for excavation and publication in Egypt and enforcing old laws that have been overlooked.

The Egyptian monuments are suffering terribly from the dangers of the modern world. They are being damaged by pollution; by wind and sand-storms; by the salt and water left behind by rising groundwater and the breath and touch of thousands of tourists, both of which eat away at the ancient stone and mud brick; and by the depredations of the tomb robbers and antiquities dealers who want to make a profit from our common heritage. The population boom in Egypt has led to more and more new construction, much of which threatens ancient sites. If we do not act now, our monuments will be gone within 100 years.

The story of archaeology in Egypt begins as a tale of foreign domination and native neglect. The balance of power has been slowly changing, but in order to ensure both the preservation of our past and the brightness of our future, it is essential that more Egyptians become informed about and proud of their heritage. Reaching out to native Egyptians, many of whom are almost completely ignorant of their own past, is a vital part of the mission of the SCA. As part of our focus on education, we will be opening a series of new museums, designed as learning and cultural centers rather than as warehouses for precious objects, around Egypt. I have also opened a new school for children in the basement of the Cairo Museum and have initiated an adult certification program so that more Egyptians can receive Egyptological training.

The opening of the school for children has fulfilled a longtime dream of mine: to provide a place to train our children while they are young to love ancient Egypt and be proud of their ancestors. I was invited recently to attend a rehearsal at the school, and I was moved to tears by the song that the children sang for all of Egypt. The faces of the children were full of the light reflected on them from the ancient past, and their minds and spirits were full of the excitement of today.

Another important focus of my work has been

Zahi Hawass opening the sarcophagus of Nesut-Wesert, Giza, Tombs of the Pyramid Builders.

the recovery of stolen artifacts. Many objects have been taken out of the country illegally over the last three decades, and both Egyptian and international antiquities laws give us the right to recover them. Stopping the trafficking of antiquities is crucial to preserving our past; we cannot allow people to continue to hoard and profit from ancient artifacts. I have set up a new department within the SCA, the Department for Recovering Stolen Antiquities, which is dedicated to pursuing this important task. We have had a number of successes so far, and will continue to catch and prosecute modern thieves.

The majority of the photographs in this book were taken by National Geographic photographer Ken Garrett, whose vision I admire. His spectacular pictures succeed in conveying the magic and mystery of ancient Egypt. He has a gift for showing ancient objects from a unique perspective, and his knowledge of ancient Egypt is considerable. We have worked together for over ten years now, and his photos and my words have often illustrated one another. Join us now as we journey through the halls and basement corridors of the Egyptian Museum in Cairo in search of our shared past and our common future.

I. from Colonialism to Nationalism

PENDANT OF THE GOD RE-HORAKHTI
Gold, carnelian, chalcedony, colored glass paste
Height 65 cm; Length 65 cm
Dynasty 18, reign of Tutankhamun
Thebes, Valley of the Kings, tomb of Tutankhamun
Carter-Carnarvon excavations, 1922–30

OUR STORY BEGINS WITH THE FOUNDING OF THE MUSEUM'S collections in the 1850s. Of course, modern interest in ancient Egypt predates this decade by several centuries. From the middle of the 17th century until the middle of the 19th century, increasingly rapacious hordes of Europeans came to Egypt and took home with them wonderful pieces of art and architecture: statues, bits of wall relief, obelisks, mummies, the treasures from great tombs—whatever they could carry.

The flood of objects leaving Egypt reached its peak in the early 1800s, after the Napoleonic expedition had come and gone, leaving vast waves of worldwide attention to Egypt and her ancient heritage in its wake. The "Rape of the Nile," as the wholesale appropriation of Egyptian antiquities by foreigners has been labeled by archaeologist and author Brian Fagan, began. There are few objects in the collections of the Egyptian Museum that were excavated during this period; almost everything went to European museums or private collections. Much of this is now gone forever; what remains is, for the most part, missing the context that accounts for a major part of its value for reconstructing the past.

In 1835 Mohamed Ali, then ruler of Egypt under the Ottomans, founded the first Egyptian Antiquities Service. He was encouraged to do this by such scholars as Jean-François Champollion, who deciphered hieroglyphs, and Rifaa al-Tahtawi, the first modern Egyptian to write about ancient Egypt. Mohamed Ali also decided to begin a collection of ancient artifacts that would stay in Egypt rather than being shipped to museums and private

collections around the world. As curator in charge of these objects he selected al-Tahtawi, a great thinker who had been educated abroad and came home in the 1820s full of enthusiasm for his country's ancient past. Under al-Tahtawi's care, the objects were placed in storerooms in the Ezbekiyeh Gardens in Cairo. But despite some glimmerings of intellectual curiosity about his country's ancient heritage, Mohamed Ali was a practical man, rooted in the present, and he gave many of the Ezbekiyeh artifacts away as diplomatic gifts.

In 1848 Mohamed Ali's successor, Khedive Abass I, moved the Ezbekiyeh artifacts to the Citadel, where they were displayed to foreign dignitaries. Several years later the next khedive, Said Pasha, showed them to Archduke Maximilian of Austria, who admired them greatly. Said Pasha immediately gave the entire lot to the archduke as a gesture of goodwill, and Egypt was once again left empty-handed.

The 19th century was a period of European colonialism and paternalism. Egypt, although nominally a part of the Ottoman Empire, was seen by various European powers as theirs to despoil. The discipline of Egyptology, officially born in the 1820s with the decipherment of the Egyptian hieroglyphic script, was no different. The French, the British, and the Germans all jockeyed for hegemony in the field and fought over whose collections at home would be the most spectacular. To be fair, a few of these men (for they were almost all male) had the best interests of the antiquities at heart and removed them to protect them and save them for posterity. But for the first half of the century, artifact collecting in Egypt was a free-for-all, with members of the elite of Europe either blatantly stealing or quietly smuggling huge numbers of spectacular objects out of the country.

There was little outcry from the Egyptians themselves, and any native interest that raised its head was quickly stamped out by European interference. Rifaa al-Tahtawi's was the lone native voice protesting the theft of his country's heritage, and he was powerless in the face of his government's desire, and indeed need, to leverage this past to ensure its present and future.

In 1850 Frenchman Auguste Mariette arrived in Egypt. His immediate goal was to buy Coptic manuscripts to take back with him to the Louvre, but he was thwarted by the Coptic patriarchy. With time on his hands, he turned his attention to the earlier periods of Egyptian history, in which he had trained extensively. Using funds originally earmarked for the manuscripts, he unearthed the Serapeum at Saqqara, tomb of the sacred Apis bulls (page 29), then took the majority of his early finds to France, against the wishes of the Egyptian government.

Khedive Abass Hilmi, during whose rule the Egyptian Museum at Tahrir Square was completed

Over time, however, Mariette changed his position and became a staunch supporter of keeping Egyptian objects in Egypt. In 1858 Khedive Said, then ruler of Egypt, founded an Antiquities Service and put this enormously energetic scholar at its head. For the next 20-odd years, Mariette excavated all over Egypt; at one point, he had teams working at 35 sites. He had permission to conscript 7,000

of what was discovered stayed in Egypt, housed in the first Egyptian Museum.

This museum was founded in 1863, under the Khedive Ismail. It was located at Boulaq, then on the edge of Cairo, across the river from Gezira Island. Its position on the banks of the river allowed heavy antiquities to be delivered via Nile barge. Archaeologists nowadays flinch at

Exterior view of the Boulaq Museum

workers, although his forces may never have reached quite this level. Most of these were poor workmen and peasants; the wealthier villagers paid bribes to the conscription officers, who then worked their way down the social ladder until they reached those who could not pay. On-site supervision was left primarily to the native *reises* (overseers) and foreign assistants. For the first time, a majority

Mariette's methods of excavation, which were far from what we would consider scientific. In addition to the fact that he was rarely present himself, his methods of documentation, although a great improvement over those of the looters who had come before him, were insufficient by modern standards; it was enough for him in many cases to list the site from which an object came. In addition, many of the more detailed records he and his assistants made were never published and have now been lost. But almost single-handedly he stopped the unchecked flow of ancient objects out of Egypt, and his prolific excavations brought many fabulous items to the Egyptian collection, several of which are featured in this book.

In 1869 the Egyptian scholar Ali Mubarak and the German Egyptologist Heinrich Brugsch established the first Egyptian school of Egyptology in a run-down villa near the Boulaq museum.

exhibits himself, arranging them according to aesthetic principles that he thought would appeal to the local visitors. By the 1870s its halls were filled to capacity, and in 1878, the museum was flooded by the Nile, destroying many of the records (including much information from Mariette's excavations) stored there and damaging many of the artifacts. Mariette responded by petitioning the authorities for a new museum at a safer, more permanent location, a request that would be granted only posthumously.

Archaeologists nowadays flinch at Mariette's methods of excavation, which were far from what we would now consider scientific.

Al-Tahtawi may also have been involved in the formation of this school. Ten Egyptian students enrolled, among them Ahmed Kamal, who would become Egypt's first native Egyptologist and later be awarded the title of pasha. Despite great success and enthusiastic support from the Ministry of Education and the viceroy himself, Mariette felt threatened, and the school lasted only five years before it closed its doors, a victim primarily of his hostility. Thus an important attempt to train Egyptian scholars in the study of their own heritage was derailed, and Kamal and his fellow scholars were forced to take positions outside the field.

The Boulaq museum was Mariette's to do with as he liked. He lived on the grounds and even had a garden there for his pet gazelle. He designed the

Mariette died in 1881 and was succeeded by another Frenchman, Gaston Maspero (1846–1916). He was a widely respected scholar and able administrator, and on his watch many remarkable finds were made in Egypt. Ahmed Kamal had not given up, even in the face of enormous opposition, and at Mariette's death petitioned to be granted a position in the Boulaq museum. He was appointed secretary and translator and later became an assistant curator. Between 1882 and 1886 Kamal was also responsible for training a group of five students in archaeology and ancient languages. His salary, however, was very small, and when the first class of students graduated, Maspero used the money earmarked for the school to pay the men as antiquities inspectors instead. In 1886 Maspero himself was forced to go back to France due to his wife's ill health, and a series of fairly incompetent Frenchmen took over the Service. The first of these, Eugène Grébaut, began his career by firing Kamal's students.

Ahmed Kamal managed to keep his position, even in the face of great opposition. It is reported that Jacques de Morgan, director of the Antiquities Service from 1892 to 1897, refused to speak to him for an entire year. Other Egyptians were not so fortunate; only Ahmed Najib, a former classmate of Kamal's, was able to find a foothold in the Service. Maspero's return to Egypt in 1899 eased the situation somewhat, but it was still very difficult for native Egyptians to be trained or hired as Egyptologists.

By 1887 the situation in the Boulaq museum was desperate, with artifacts stacked against walls or on top of one another, or simply stored on boats near the sites where they were found. Finally, the Khedive Ismail donated one of his palaces at Giza, on the current site of the Giza zoo, to be used as a new museum. Grébaut was in charge of moving the objects from Boulaq to Giza, but perhaps because of his incompetence as an administrator, many of them disappeared en route. The Giza museum was not large enough to hold and display the collections adequately, so in 1890 the Khedive Tawfiq, Ismail's son and successor, decided to build a new museum in downtown Cairo. An international competition was held and a French architect chosen to design the museum. Italians were awarded the construction contract.

The foundations of the new museum were laid in 1897, to great international acclaim. By March 1902 the building was almost ready, and objects began to be transported to it from the Giza museum, Boulaq, and Ezbekiyeh. In November of that year, the museum was ready to be opened to the public.

The era between the opening of the museum and World War I was characterized by infighting between the French, who controlled the Antiquities Service, and the British, who claimed Egypt as a colonial possession. Foreign scholars dominated the field of Egyptology. Chief among these was British archaeologist William Flinders Petrie, known as the Father of Egyptian Archaeology. Petrie first came to Egypt in the late 1800s, seeking scientific support for the ideas of Piazzi Smythe, astronomer royal of Scotland, who believed that the measurements of the Great Pyramid held the key to arcane secrets of the past and future. At the age of almost 30, Petrie arrived at Giza and began taking his own detailed measurements, hoping to

Egyptian archaeologists and dignitaries pose at Saqqara, 1936. In the center, seated, with his coat on his lap, is Selim Hassan; to Hassan's left is Zakaria Ghoneim.

prove Smythe's theory correct and silence his detractors. It was not long, however, before the young genius realized that his mentor was misguided. Rapidly becoming fascinated with ancient Egypt for its own sake, and having an enormously methodical turn of mind, Petrie began his own research, supported by a number of institutions, at various sites around Egypt. Excavations before Petrie were still primarily treasure hunts, in the vein of *Raiders of the Lost Ark*. Petrie instituted new methods of digging and recording and insisted on paying attention to all finds, whether large or small. He was especially interested in pottery and was able

to use the many potsherds he found to help him date the sites on which he worked. Also important was Maspero, who inaugurated the great Catalogue General of the Cairo Museum. We will meet some of these men and other key archaeologists of the period through some of the objects that they brought to the museum.

Against great odds, Kamal and fellow scholar Ahmed Lufti Al-Sayyid tried to break down the barriers of prejudice and fear that had long kept native Egyptians out of the field of Egyptology. Ahmed Najib gave up the fight and left Egyptology for journalism in 1905. In 1910 Kamal persuaded the

Ministry of Education to let him create an Egyptology section in the Higher Teachers College of Cairo; the first class graduated in 1912, but the program was discontinued in 1913. Despite Kamal's best efforts, his students were unable to secure jobs with the Antiquities Service, and were forced to teach high school to make ends meet. However, Kamal also taught courses on ancient Egypt at the Egyptian University, and he and several of his fellow native Egyptologists began publishing in Arabic. Their goal was to promote the love of Egyptian heritage among Egyptians; their books mark the beginning of an increased awareness of and pride in the ancient past within Egypt's native population.

This period saw a continuation of the pillaging of Egypt's past by foreigners. Anyone with enough money and influence could be granted a *firman* (permission to excavate), regardless of his skill or knowledge. Officially, artifacts were to be divided between Egypt and the organization or person funding the excavations, with Egypt getting preference for great works of art. However, theory and practice did not always correspond, and major artifacts still left the country. The antiquities trade continued to thrive, so many objects also left the country illegally.

In 1922, after the horrors of the First World War, Britain gave Egypt nominal independence, and the Antiquities Service (still run by foreigners) had a somewhat better chance of controlling the antiquities trade. This was also an important year for Egyptology due to the discovery by Englishman Howard Carter of the tomb of Tutankhamun, which fascinated people around the world. It was truly the beginning of a new era, for Ahmed Kamal, who retired in 1914, died only months after the discovery of the tomb. Another important milestone was the founding of a school of archaeology dedicated to the training of Egyptian Egyptologists.

The tomb of Tuankhamun had lain undisturbed since remote antiquity. Because it was basically an intact royal tomb, Pierre Lacau, then director of the Antiquities Service, insisted that all of its contents remain in Egypt. The resulting struggle between Carter and the Service led to the issuing of a new antiquities law in 1926, which claimed the majority of finds for Egypt and marked an important turning point in the history of Egyptian archaeology. Instead of being able to keep some of the important artifacts they found, archaeologists and the institutions that supported them were forced to be satisfied with taking with them only minor pieces and the information they extracted from their sites.

> Anyone with enough money and influence could be granted a *firman* (permission to excavate), regardless of his skill or knowledge.

Many gave up. Petrie, for example, whose expeditions had been funded by European museums that traded financial support for antiquities, left Egypt for Palestine, and did not return.

Important foreign Egyptologists of this period included: the American scholar and scientific archaeologist George Reisner (1867–1942); Hermann Junker (1877–1962), a German who had

for Egyptian archaeologists, such as Selim Hassan (1886–1961), to rise to key positions within the Service and carry out important excavations, although they still had to face enormous foreign opposition and prejudice. Hassan, a student of Kamal's and a key member of the first generation of Egyptian excavators, worked at Giza and Saqqara, and earned a doctorate from Vienna in 1939.

Zaki Youssef Saad, Walter Bryan Emery, Makramallah, Pierre Lacau, and Jean-Philippe Lauer at the Saqqara Inspectorate, 1935

originally intended to become a priest; and Ludwig Borchardt (1863–1938), who excavated at Abusir and Amarna.

In the 1930s, the newly powerful Antiquities Service took control of exportation, museums, antiquities, schools, and the training of new Egyptian Egyptologists. It finally became possible

We will now travel back through time, visiting the excavations of Mariette, Petrie, Hassan, and others. Through the spectacular objects that are illustrated in these pages, we will learn about the early days of archaeology in Egypt and catch scattered glimpses of this period of foreign ascendency and native struggle.

STELA OF PADISET
Limestone
Height 11 cm; Width 7.6 cm
Late period
Saqqara, Serapeum
Excavations of August Mariette, 1851

AFTER HIS REQUEST FOR COPTIC MANUSCRIPTS TO PURCHASE WAS denied by the church hierarchy, Auguste Mariette became interested in the vast necropolis at Saqqara and spent much of his time exploring the many tombs still visible on its surface. One day he came upon a sphinx half buried in the sand and recognized it as the twin of several that he had already noticed in Cairo and Alexandria. This one was clearly in its original place, and others like it were nearby. Mariette remembered a passage in the writings of the first century B.C. Greek author Strabo that mentioned an avenue of sphinxes at Saqqara leading to the Serapeum, the burial place of the sacred Apis bulls. Without applying to the pasha for permission, Mariette gathered together a crew of workers and began to clear the path made by the sphinxes. Several weeks of digging led him to the underground burial vaults where the Apis bulls were entombed in a complex of chambers and galleries.

The Apis bulls were sacred to the god Ptah, patron god of Memphis and god of artisans. There was one Apis bull at a time, carefully chosen through very specific criteria. During its lifetime, each bull was worshiped in a special temple built of mud brick; at its death, it was mummified and placed within an elaborate nest of coffins and sarcophagi, then, with great ceremony, buried in an underground vault beneath the temple, along with specially made funerary furniture. The first bull burials, beginning in the reign of Amenhotep III, took place in isolated chambers. Ramses II (circa 1279 B.C. to 1213 B.C.) began an underground gallery, now known as the Lesser Vaults, with large alcoves carved to each side in which the sacred bulls were laid to rest. A second corridor, the Greater Vaults, was later carved at right angles to this one.

At the main entrance to the vaults is a wall full of niches, where officials connected with the burials of the bulls and visitors to the chambers left votive stelae. Mariette recovered more than 1,200 stelae from this area, spanning the years from the late New Kingdom (circa 1390 B.C.) to the end of the Ptolemaic era (31 B.C.). Some of these were royal monuments, but most, like the one shown here, were dedicated by the workmen and officials involved with the burials of the divine bulls. This is a typical example. The Apis bull, identified as divine by the sun disk between its horns, stands on a low pedestal. Before it kneels Padiset, the man who has dedicated this small relief. By placing a stela in the Serapeum, this man, one in a long line of priests, associated himself with the cult of the divine bull for eternity.

Of the 1,200 such stelae that were found by Mariette, most were taken to the Louvre; only 400 were put into the Boulaq museum. However, many of these were given away by Said Pasha as gifts to visiting dignitaries, and others were damaged in the 1878 flood. Only 30 of Mariette's stelae remain in the collection of the Cairo Museum.

UNDERGROUND VAULT OF THE SERAPEUM, SAQQARA

1859: Tomb of the Warrior Queen

IN FEBRUARY 1859 A TEAM OF WORKMEN NOMINALLY UNDER THE supervision of Mariette were working in the Dra Abu el-Naga section of the Theban necropolis when they stumbled across the intact burial of a queen named Ahhotep. Ahhotep lived at the end of the Second Intermediate period, a time when the north of Egypt was occupied and ruled by foreigners known as the Hyksos. Native princes of the 17th dynasty, based at Thebes, held sway in the south as vassals of the Hyksos until the reign of Ahhotep's husband, Seqenenere Tao II, who began the war to expel the hated Hyksos and reunite the country. Seqenenere Tao II died in battle, judging from the wounds in the shape of Asiatic axes still visible in the skull of his mummy, and his elder son, Kamose, took over as war leader. Kamose fought hard and bravely to defeat the Hyksos but died before he could finish the task. Queen Ahhotep was left as queen-regent until her younger son, Ahmose, was of age and could finish driving the foreign invaders from Egyptian soil.

Queen Ahhotep was found inside her original coffin, shown here, which was made of an expensive imported wood overlaid with gold leaf, the eyes inlaid with alabaster and obsidian. With Ahhotep was a rich cache of funerary equipment, including weapons and three golden flies strung onto a necklace—a traditional Egyptian military decoration. She also took into the afterlife objects bearing the names of her two sons, Kamose and Ahmose.

When the queen was found, the local authorities did not wait for Mariette but ordered that she and her goods be taken from the safety of her tomb and delivered to them. They immediately opened the coffin and ripped apart the mummy, looking for gold and jewels, which they found in significant quantity; the now destroyed mummy, along with its wrappings, was tossed into the trash. Gathering together the results of this vandalism, the local pasha sent the whole lot off to Said Pasha, then ruler of Egypt, in Cairo. Furious at being bypassed, and justifiably worried that the golden hoard would be melted down or given away, Mariette jumped into his official steamer and headed south for Thebes. When he reached the treasure-filled boat, which was sailing north, he pulled alongside and harangued the crew, threatening them with all sorts of dire physical abuse, until they finally agreed to give him the precious antiquities.

The treasures of Ahhotep stand as a tribute to Mariette's dedication to keeping monuments of the pharaonic past within Egypt's own borders. In 1867 Empress Eugénie (the wife of Napoleon III) asked for the queen's jewels as a gift. Although Ismail Pasha, who was then ruler of Egypt, was willing to part with the treasure, Mariette refused, at the cost of the enormous displeasure of both Ismail and the French royal house.

STATUE OF KING KHAFRE
Diorite
Height 168 cm
Dynasty 4, reign of Khafre
Giza, Valley Temple of Khafre
Excavations of Mariette, 1860

1860: God Kings of Giza

IN 1860 ONE OF MARIETTE'S TEAMS WAS WORKING AT GIZA, IN A STRUCTURE that was later identified as the Valley Temple of Khafre. Each pyramid complex had such a temple lying at or close to the border between floodplain and desert, connecting the realm of the living with the kingdom of the dead. The walls of this beautiful temple are lined with monolithic slabs of shining red granite, and the floor is paved with irregular alabaster slabs, fitted together with exquisite precision. In the entrance hall, the workers found a large pit, inside which lay the remains of seven of the twenty-three statues that had once lined the inner sanctuary of this magnificent temple. Five were badly damaged, but two, including this one, were relatively intact. I believe that these were hidden here during the First Intermediate period, the era following the end of the Old Kingdom. This was a time of great chaos, with no strong centralized government to maintain control, and a great deal of anger raged against the kings who had come before. The monuments at Giza were vandalized at this time, the treasures of the kings ransacked and their temples destroyed. The statues that stood in Khafre's temples appear to have been smashed in vengeful anger. After the Valley Temple of Khafre was attacked, loyal priests may have buried what remained, trying to save what they could from the vandals who would surely return.

This statue is one of the masterpieces of Egyptian art, a centerpiece of the Egyptian Museum. It is carved from diorite, which was extracted from the earth far to the south of Egypt, in Khafre's Nubian quarries. Old Kingdom graffiti, which include the cartouche of this great king, have been found in these quarries, showing a clear link between Nubia and Giza, the location of the workshop where this statue was created.

No one who sees this statue could doubt for a moment that it is meant to represent a king. The artist has breathed life into the hard stone, making the royal blood seem to flow beneath the youthful muscles. The king is seen here as Osiris, first king of Egypt and ruler of the realm of the dead. The throne upon which he is seated represents the hieroglyphic name of Osiris's wife, Isis. If you look at the statue from the side, you will see that behind Khafre's head hovers a hawk that embraces him and seems to carry him to the sky; this hawk is Horus, son of Osiris and Isis and eternal ruler of the Two Lands. Thus the statue is both an image of the king and a symbol of one of the principal divine triads of the ancient Egyptians.

STELA OF LADY SENETITES
Limestone
Height 65 cm; Width 32.5 cm
Dynasty 12 to 13
Abydos
Collected by Mariette, 1881

1881: Terrace of the Great God at Abydos

DEEP IN THE HEART OF EGYPT LIES THE SACRED SITE OF ABYDOS, CULT center of Osiris, the mythical first king of Egypt and god of the dead. Archaeological ruins spanning the entire pharaonic period litter the sands that lie between the brooding cliffs of the high desert and the fertile floodplain. The first kings of Egypt were buried here, in tombs that lay far out in the western desert at a site known as the Umm el-Qa'ab ("Mother of Pots," so named because of the potsherds that cover the surface of the sands like a carpet). Closer to the cultivation were huge mortuary complexes surrounded by towering, elaborately niched walls of mud brick, calling to mind the rectangles bordered at the bottom by patterned niches in which the names of kings were written from the earliest times (known as *serekhs*). One of these enclosures, dating to the reign of the last king of the 2nd dynasty, Khasekhemwy, still stands today, dominating the desert landscape.

In the Old Kingdom, a temple to the mortuary god Khenti-imentiu (Foremost of the Westerners) flourished here, and a ritual voyage to Abydos, whether real or symbolic, became part of an ideal funeral. During the Middle Kingdom, this ancient site gained in importance in conjunction with the rise of the cult of Osiris, with whom Khenti-imentiu was merged. The tomb of one of the kings of the 1st dynasty was identified as the grave of this god. An annual festival was held at Abydos to honor Osiris, and many people set up stelae to ensure that they would share eternally in the celebration and its associated offerings. In the New Kingdom, both Seti I and his son, Ramses II, built beautiful temples at the edge of the floodplain.

The area where many of these votive stelae, often housed within mud-brick mortuary chapels, were erected was called the Terrace of the Great God. Mariette sent a team to this area and collected many of these monuments for the Boulaq museum. This is one of the most beautiful. It was dedicated by a man named Khnumu for his daughter, Senetites. The central panel follows the development of the Old Kingdom false door (page 140), depicting the cult recipient seated at a table piled high with offerings. Senetites holds a lotus, symbol of resurrection, in one hand; under her chair are a cosmetic box and a maidservant with a mirror. The inscription above Senetites' head asks that offerings be made for her in perpetuity.

1871: The Hidden Pair

Painted limestone
Height of Rahotep 121 cm
Height of Nofret 122 cm
Dynasty 4, reign of Sneferu
Meidum, mastaba of Rahotep and
  Nofret
Mariette excavations, 1871

IN SEPTEMBER 1871 A TEAM FIELDED BY AN ALEXANDRIAN MERCHANT named Vigne was working at Meidum, searching for ancient animal remains, when they found the edge of a large stela. The observant headman of the nearby village realized that this was part of a still buried structure that should be explored properly and sent a message to the authorities. Mariette could not come but sent his deputy, Albert Daninos, in his stead. The letter of instruction sent by Mariette to Daninos is very specific, telling him to leave everything in place and record whatever he finds with great care.

Daninos arrived at Meidum, location of one of the pyramids of Sneferu—first king of the 4th dynasty and one of the greatest pyramid builders in history—in late December. His first task was to investigate the stela, which he identified as belonging to a prince named Rahotep and his wife, Nofret. Clearance of the surrounding sand exposed the face of a mastaba built of mud brick and lined with limestone. Behind the stela was a niche sealed with two blocks of limestone; there was no doorway into the interior of the tomb chapel. Daninos brought in a stonemason, who broke through the first two blocks and then through a series of six more before he reached a small tunnel. Taking a candle with him, the mason crawled into the narrow passage, only to reappear several minutes later overcome with terror. Gabbling with fear, he told Daninos that there were two people staring out at him from inside a hidden chamber. My Egyptian sources, who heard the story from their grandparents and their grandparents' grandparents, tell me that once he had calmed down from the original shock, the stonemason became so excited about the prospect of the tip he would earn as a result of this discovery that he died of a heart attack. Daninos, who was calmer (and forewarned), crawled through the tunnel himself and found the two exquisite statues seen here.

Rahotep was a high official in Sneferu's government and was probably the king's brother. Among his other duties, he served as High Priest at the temple of the sun god in Iunu (now called Heliopolis and known in the Bible as On), and was commander in chief of the Egyptian army. His wife was a member of the court. Their important position in the society of the 4th dynasty is reflected in the extraordinarily high quality of the carving and painting of these beautiful statues, which were carved of limestone and then painted, their eyes inlaid with alabaster and quartz. Very little private statuary dating from the reign of Sneferu's son, Khufu, has been found. Some scholars believe that Khufu issued a decree banning private people from placing statues in their tombs. The fact that the statues of Rahotep and Nofret were hidden behind a wall of limestone may have been the result of this hypothetical decree—perhaps Rahotep ordered the statues made in secret, and then hid them away.

1881: The Royal Mummies of Deir el-Bahri

ONE OF THE GREATEST OF THE DISCOVERIES FROM GASTON MASPERO'S tenure as head of the Antiquities Service was made by a local family from the west bank of Thebes. The Abd el-Rassoul family had lived near the Valley of the Kings as far back as anyone could remember. Their ancestors may have been the men who carved and painted the royal tombs, and also the men who robbed them. According to legend, one day in the summer of 1871 Ahmed Abd el-Rassoul was tending his goats in the rocky Theban hills when one of his charges ran away. Following it, Ahmed found himself at the top of a shaft 30 meters deep (98 feet), one of many that honeycomb the area. He lowered himself down by rope to the corridor of a coffin-filled tomb. The family soon realized that they had stumbled across the final resting place of many of the greatest pharaohs of the New Kingdom, whose mummies had been taken from their original tombs by priests of the 21st dynasty, rewrapped, and buried in this remote tomb for safekeeping. With the bodies were whatever bits of funerary furniture had been left behind by the ancient thieves (and by the priests themselves, who are thought to have taken some objects for use by the current rulers).

Exercising caution, the modern robbers entered the tomb only three times over the next ten years. They brought out a few of the fabulous artifacts and slowly leaked them onto the antiquities market. But objects bearing important royal names could not escape official notice for long. Several royal wooden statuettes being sold in Paris came to the attention of Gaston Maspero, who traveled to Luxor to try to find their source. He discovered that the Abd el-Rassoul family was responsible, and Ahmed Abd el-Rassoul was put in jail. Despite intense interrogation, Ahmed refused to talk. After his release, Ahmed went home and asked for a greater share of the treasure as a reward for his stoicism. The family refused, and his brother Mohammed, afraid that Ahmed would betray them, revealed the location of the hidden cache to the police.

The Antiquities Service quickly descended upon the tomb, led by Emile Brugsch (brother of Heinrich Brugsch); Egyptian scholar Ahmed Kamal played a key role in supervising the work and dealing with the Theban villagers. The mummies and their remaining goods were quickly recorded, taken from the tomb, and loaded onto a boat bound for Cairo. When the boat arrived in Cairo, the customs officers did not know how to classify the royal remains and listed them in the official register as salted fish.

The mummies seen here are two of the greatest pharaohs ever to govern Egypt: Seti I and his son Ramses II. These two men ruled during the 19th dynasty, during the last days of power of one of the greatest empires the world has ever seen. With their fellow monarchs, they rest now in a special room at the Cairo Museum. Later, they will be transferred to the National Museum at Fustat, where they will be displayed in an updated exhibit.

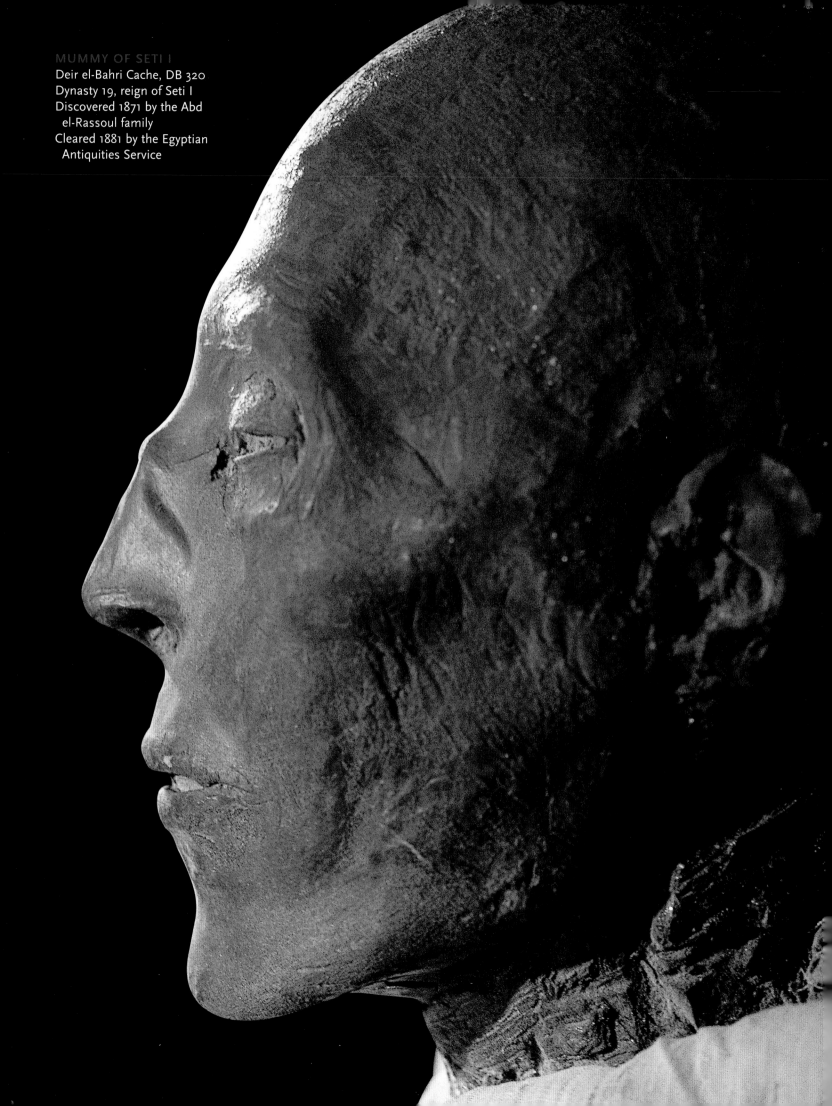

MUMMY OF RAMSES II
Deir el-Bahri Cache, DB 320
Dynasty 19, reign of Ramses II
Discovered 1871 by the Abd el-Rassoul family
Cleared 1881 by the Egyptian Antiquities Service

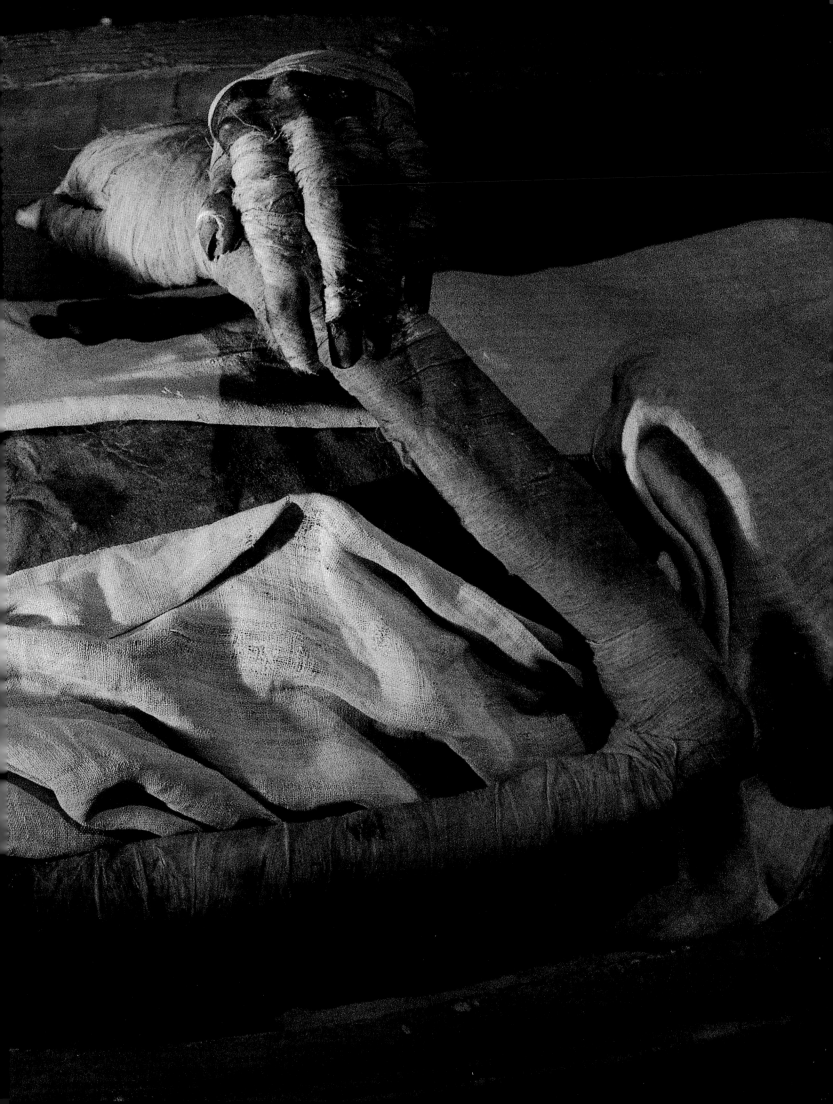

MUMMY MASKS OF SENNEDJEM (LEFT) AND HIS WIFE (ABOVE)
Painted cartonnage
Sennedjem: Height 45 cm; Width 28 cm
Wife: Height 52 cm; Width 28 cm
Dynasty 19 (1318–1304 B.C.)
Deir el-Medineh, Tomb of Sennedjem
Abu Duhi; expeditions of the Egyptian
  Antiquities Service (Gaston Maspero),
  1886

THE WORKMEN WHO HOLLOWED OUT AND THEN DECORATED THE ROYAL tombs in the Valley of the Kings lived in a town on the western bank of Thebes known as Deir el-Medineh. This site was most likely founded in the reign of Thutmosis I (circa 1493 B.C.) and occupied continuously for about 500 years. The valley of the royal tombs was known to the ancients as the Place of Truth, and the workers were called Servants in the Place of Truth. Because of its location in the desert, Deir el-Medineh survived the passing of the eons remarkably well. Important literary, administrative, and personal texts, including the transcripts of trials and other legal proceedings, were recovered in considerable number from this site, and scholars have been able to build up a highly nuanced picture of life here in ancient times. The town and its associated necropolis was well known as a rich vein of antiquities by the early 1800s and was thoroughly raided by early explorers. But the careless and far from systematic looters left much of value behind them, to be discovered later by chance or design.

Once Maspero had succeeded Mariette, it was much easier for both foreign and native missions to gain permission to excavate. In 1886 Salam Abu Duhi, a villager from Gurneh (the modern village nearby), was granted a concession to explore an area of Deir el-Medineh near his house. After only a few days of work, he, with three friends, made a spectacular discovery: At the bottom of a previously unexplored tomb shaft was a closed wooden door, its ancient seals still unbroken. He reported the find immediately to Maspero, who happened to be in Luxor at the time on his annual tour of inspection. The next day, Maspero and several colleagues followed Abu Duhi down into the newly discovered tomb. Fighting to breathe in the hot and airless corridor, the team carefully removed the door and entered the chamber, the first humans to do so in 3,000 years. The walls of the chamber inside were exquisitely painted with scenes of the afterlife, and on the floor, accompanied by their funerary furnishings, were 20 bodies: 9 in wooden coffins, and 11 others scattered about haphazardly.

The owner of the tomb was Sennedjem, a workman who lived during the reign of Seti I and was probably one of the artisans who built this monarch's magnificent tomb. The tomb of Sennedjem is one of the most beautiful nonroyal tombs to be found in the region. The burial chamber is small, with a vaulted ceiling, and every detail of the predominantly golden paintings that cover its walls is exquisitely done. As a royal artisan, Sennedjem would have been able to barter with his fellow workers: The funerary masks of Sennedjem and his wife, shown here, demonstrate the high artistic quality of both the tomb itself and the objects found within it.

1888: Priest of the Past

THE MEMPHITE REGION LIES AT THE APEX OF THE NILE DELTA, AT A POINT where the Nile Valley, the northern floodplain, and a number of important desert trade routes converge. Ancient historical sources tell us that a capital was founded in the area by the first king of the 1st dynasty, and royalty and high officials from the Early Dynastic period built their tombs at the nearby site of Saqqara. The kings of both the Old and Middle Kingdoms constructed their pyramids in the area, in a line stretching from Abu Rawash in the north to Meidum in the south. In the New Kingdom, Memphis (called Men-nefer in ancient Egyptian, after the name of an Old Kingdom pyramid) was considered one of the major capitals of Egypt, along with Thebes in the south and, in the later New Kingdom, Piramesse in the north.

Settlement remains from the New Kingdom have been found in an area known as Mit Rahina, where there are a number of structures, including small temples dedicated to Ptah—patron god of the area—and Hathor by Ramses II; a huge precinct for Ptah, also built primarily by this king; and a palace complex designed by Ramses II's successor, Merneptah. Until recently, there was no good evidence for a town or city here before the First Intermediate period. New excavations being carried out by David Jefferies at the foot of the Saqqara escarpment, immediately north of the Early Dynastic tombs, are finally revealing traces of an Archaic settlement.

This squat statue of hard granite was reportedly found at Mit Rahina, but no details of its discovery are available. The awkwardly carved image represents a priest named Hetepdief, son of Merydjehuty. Despite its somewhat unprepossessing appearance, this statue is extremely important. It has been dated, on stylistic grounds, to the latter part of the 2nd or beginning of the 3rd dynasty (circa 2650 B.C.). On Hetepdief's right shoulder are carved three "palace facades," or serekhs, rectangles surmounted by Horus falcons and bordered at the bottom by a pattern representing the niches that would have decorated the walls of the royal palace. Inside each serekh is the name of a 2nd dynasty king; thus, Hetepdief is assumed to have been involved in some way with their cults. The fact that there is little information available about the discovery of this statue underlines the chaos that still prevailed in Egypt in the late 19th century. Much irreplaceable information was lost when this statue was casually collected and brought to the museum, and left unpublished by its discoverer. Was this originally placed in Hetepdief's tomb? Or was it, as the kneeling posture of the priest might suggest, a votive image, placed in a temple? This is one of the earliest examples of private sculpture known from ancient Egypt, and information about where and how it was found would make this rare piece even more valuable.

Left: Gold, carnelian, turquoise, and lapis lazuli
Right: Gold, carnelian, turquoise, amethyst, and lapis lazuli
Left: Height of pectoral 7.9 cm; Width 10.5 cm
Right: Height of pectoral 6.1 cm; Width 8.6 cm
Dynasty 12, reigns of Amenemhat III and Senwosret III
Dahshur, complex of Senwosret III, tomb of Mereret
Excavations of Jacques de Morgan, 1894

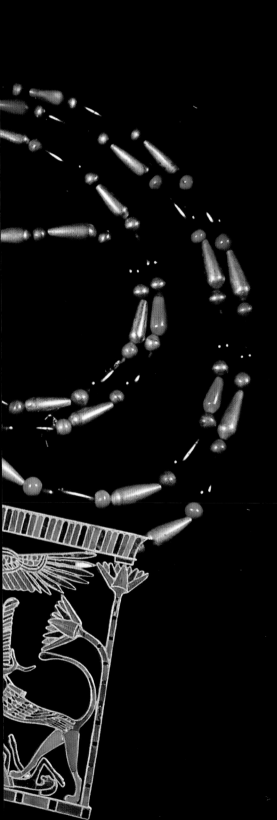

IN 1893 JACQUES DE MORGAN, WHO WAS THEN HEAD OF THE ANTIQUITIES Service, decided to begin work at the site of Dahshur, location of the two pyramids of Sneferu, father of Khufu, and of several pyramids belonging to Middle Kingdom rulers. De Morgan was a businessman with no training in Egyptology, but he seems to have been a great improvement over his predecessor, Eugène Grébaut. The site of Dahshur was known to contain numerous tombs, and the remains of the great pyramids in various stages of decay were easily visible on the surface. Some excavation had been carried out earlier at the site, but no systematic exploration had yet been undertaken. On March 7, 1894, as de Morgan was working at the northwest corner of the pyramid of Senwosret III, he came across a vertical shaft set to the east of four small pyramids. The shaft led to two galleries, and in the lower of these he discovered the jewels of Princess Sithathor hidden inside a pit. The next day de Morgan found a second cache, in a similar location, in the tomb of a princess named Mereret. Included in these caches of jewels were pectorals bearing the names of three important 12th dynasty kings: Senwosret II, Senwosret III (the father of Princess Mereret), and Amenemhat III (her brother). These were accompanied by many other beautiful items of gold and semiprecious stones. The burials of the two women had been plundered in antiquity, but the thieves had overlooked these caches of treasure.

The next year de Morgan was even more fortunate and found three intact burials that the ancient thieves had missed. The jewels found with these royal mummies—two princesses and a queen—were perhaps even more spectacular than the ones he had found the year before. And more Middle Kingdom gold remained to be found. Over the course of the hundred years since this discovery, several more caches have been found, and more may still lie hidden beneath the sands of the desert.

The two necklaces with attached pectorals illustrated were most likely gifts from Mereret's father and brother. The pectoral on the left shows Senwosret III in the traditional pose of the victorious pharaoh, smiting his enemies. The throne name of Amenemhat III, Nimaatre, is written inside the two cartouches, which flank hieroglyphs that name him as "the good god, lord of the two lands and all the foreign countries." Above the scene hovers the vulture-goddess Nekhbet, protectress of the king. The theme of the pectoral on the right is basically the same: Nekhbet protects images of the king as a falcon-headed sphinx trampling the enemies of Egypt. In this case, the name in the cartouche is Khakaure, the throne name of Senwosret III.

1895: The Double of the King

KA STATUE OF KING AUIBRE-HOR
Wood, gold leaf, semiprecious stones
Height 1.70 m for statue;
  2.07 m for naos
Dynasty 13, reign of Auibre-Hor
Dahshur, pyramid complex of
  Amenemhat III, tomb of Auibre-Hor
Excavations of the Egyptian Antiquities
  Service (de Morgan), 1895

BY APRIL 1895 DE MORGAN HAD MOVED THE SITE OF HIS EXPLORATIONS AT Dahshur to the area around the pyramid of Amenemhat III, known as the black pyramid. Excavating near the northeast corner of the main pyramid, he came across a deep shaft leading to two small subterranean chambers. Fragments of a badly damaged wooden statue and two alabaster vases found near the surface of the shaft bore inscriptions identifying the occupant of the tomb as a king, Auibre-Hor. This king is not known from any other sources, and it is generally assumed that he was a minor king of the late 12th or early 13th dynasty. In one of the chambers was the body of the king inside its coffin; in the other was this statue, enclosed within its *naos,* or small shrine, covered by a mass of staffs and pots. When the statue was found, it was blanketed with a fine layer of gray paint, but this disintegrated at the first modern touch. Traces of gold leaf still cling to the body, indicating that some parts would have been covered by this precious metal. Although he is now naked, the king might once have worn a kilt; he once also held a scepter in one hand and a staff in the other. The hieroglyphic sign for *ka* mounted on the head of this life-size image tells us that it represents the creative life force of the king. This was an essential part of every being, whether human or divine, and was created at the same time as the individual. Each person was accompanied throughout life by his or her ka; the ka was the part of the individual that survived death and was able to receive magical nourishment from offerings made to the deceased. The long, curled beard worn by this statue is a marker of divinity. This piece was moved to the new Cairo Museum in 1902 but then disappeared. It was later found in a corner of the museum, where apparently it had been hidden by a workman who had damaged it and wanted to avoid punishment.

Limestone
Height 75 cm; Width 44 cm;
 Depth 44 cm
Dynasty 19, reign of Ramses II
Thebes, Ramesseum
Excavations of W. M. F. Petrie, 1896

1896: The White Queen

IN 1896 WILLIAM FLINDERS PETRIE WAS EXCAVATING A CHAPEL NEAR THE mortuary temple of Ramses II at Thebes when he discovered this beautiful but damaged limestone statue, of which only the top part remains. Since a name was not preserved on the statue, she was nicknamed the White Queen. Petrie could not identify her and even thought she might date to the 26th dynasty. However, subsequent scholars suggested that this was an image of Merytamun, daughter-wife of Ramses II. In the 1980s, nearly a century after the discovery of this piece, a statue almost identical to this one but ten times larger was found by accident at Akhmim, cult center of the god Min. It lay 50 meters (165 feet) in front of a recently discovered colossal limestone statue depicting Ramses II seated on a throne. Thus the date and identity of the White Queen were confirmed.

Ramses II ruled Egypt for 66 years, outliving many of his 100 children and eight wives. At the death of his principal wife, Nefertari, Merytamun, along with one of her sisters, was advanced to the rank of Great Royal Wife. Several kings before Ramses II are known to have married their daughters; royal women played a number of important cultic roles in the royal rituals that helped to maintain the proper functioning of the cosmos. Although there is still debate as to the exact characteristics of the relationship between this great pharaoh and his beautiful daughters, the primary impetus for this marriage would have been religious. We see Merytamun here in her guise as priestess of Hathor, patroness of music and love and one of the chief goddesses in the Egyptian pantheon.

1897–1898: City of the Falcon

PLUMED FALCON HEAD
Gold and obsidian
Height 37.5 cm
Old Kingdom, Dynasty 6
Hierakonpolis, Temple of Horus
Excavations of J. E. Quibell and F. W.
 Green, 1897–98

TWO OF THE NEW BREED OF ARCHAEOLOGISTS INFLUENCED BY PETRIE were James Edward Quibell (1867–1935)—who went on to have a stellar career in Egyptian archaeology, including a stint as head of the Cairo Museum—and Frederick William Green. From 1897 to 1899 they worked at the ancient site of Nekhen, known to the Greeks as Hierakonpolis and today called el-Kom el-Ahmar. This town, sacred to the falcon-god Horus, was an important administrative and religious center as early as 5,000 years ago, when the Egyptian state was first founded. The site of Hierakonpolis had been worked over a great deal before Quibell and Green arrived, and much of the town mound had been carried away for fertilizer (a common, and ongoing, problem at many Egyptian sites). Much important information was uncovered, although it was generally not well recorded. The earliest decorated tomb in Egypt was excavated here, but its location has since been lost.

Digging in the southern part of the town mound, Quibell and Green came across the remains of a temple whose earliest phase dated to about 3000 B.C.; this is the earliest god's temple known from ancient Egypt. This golden hawk's head, part of a cult statue, emerged from the Old Kingdom levels of the temple. In the middle of a series of five chambers had been dug a pit into which this image had been placed, apparently for safekeeping or as part of the ritual burial of old cult equipment. When first discovered, the copper body of the hawk was still intact, but exposure to the air caused it to disintegrate in moments. The glistening eyes of this divine bird are made of obsidian (in fact, a single bar runs through the head), and the plumes above its head are of hammered gold and may date to a later period than the hawk itself, which is believed to be from the 6th dynasty (circa 2250 B.C.). This beautiful object was recently restored, and is now on display as part of the Hidden Treasures exhibit.

COPPER STATUES OF PEPI I

Beaten copper, limestone, and obsidian
Large statue: Height 177 cm
Small statue: Height 65 cm
Old Kingdom, Dynasty 6, reign of Pepi I
Hierakonpolis, Temple of Horus
Excavation of Quibell and Green, 1897–98

IN ANOTHER CHAMBER OF THE SAME TEMPLE WHERE THE FALCON WAS discovered, Quibell and Green uncovered a life-size statue of copper. A sheet of copper on its chest identified it as Pepi I, a king of the 6th dynasty (circa 2250 B.C.). To the great surprise of the archaeologists, when they looked inside the statue's trunk they found a second, smaller statue, long thought to be the image of Pepi I's son and successor, Merenre, although there is also a fairly convincing school of thought that identifies both statues as likenesses of Pepi I himself. The identifying inscription associates the statues with Pepi I's Sed festival, an important event celebrated for the first time after 30 years of rule. The festival, often nicknamed the Jubilee, is still incompletely understood, but it is generally thought to have been designed to renew the kingship and celebrate the king's accomplishments. Thus the small statue could be either Pepi I himself after his rejuvenation or Merenre, placed on the throne as his co-regent on the occasion of his festival. The eyes of the statues are inlaid with limestone and obsidian; additional details were picked out in gold, most of which has worn away. Other parts of the statues—such as the larger statue's crown, the small statue's *uraeus* (the royal cobra that graced its forehead), and the kilts worn by both—were made of different materials, and are now lost.

At the time of their discovery, the statues were in pieces and were terribly corroded. Some conservation was carried out by an Italian named Barsanti, who was once known by the nickname Baracementi because he used cement in most of his restorations. Over the decades since their discovery, the statues continued to decay slowly. In 1996 the German Institute in Cairo, with impetus from Rainer Stadelmann, spearheaded a joint conservation project with the Römisch-Germanisches Zentralmuseum Mainz and the SCA to begin restoration of these beautiful pieces. The pieces were moved into a lab at the museum, where they were carefully treated by Christian Eckmann and Saher Shafik. Before any work was done, the statues were x-rayed and studied carefully. The scans revealed new cracks, and careful analysis showed that some of the fragments had been reconstructed incorrectly—for example, a fragment of the torso of the smaller figure had been included in its foot. Both statues were carefully cleaned of all corrosives and other residue and treated with a solution to neutralize the salt that was eating away at the metal. Studies carried out by the conservation team have provided new insights into the techniques used to create these masterpieces. Although I admit that I miss the way the statues looked before, which gave one a sense of how ancient they are, they have now regained more of their original appearance and are better conserved for the future.

1898–99: More Royal Mummies

MUMMY OF MERENPTAH

Valley of the Kings, Tomb of
  Amenhotep II
Excavations of the Egyptian Antiquities
  Service (Victor Loret), 1898–99

JACQUES DE MORGAN LEFT EGYPT IN 1897, AND VICTOR LORET (1859–1946) took his place as director of the Antiquities Service. This French Egyptologist, who by most accounts was quite difficult to get along with, stayed at this post for only two years. His short tenure, however, was marked by the spectacular discovery of 17 new tombs in the Valley of the Kings, and by the creation of the *Annales du Service,* still the official journal of the SCA. The second royal tomb discovered by Loret's workers (with help from one of the Abd el-Rassoul brothers) was KV35, the tomb of Amenhotep II (circa 1426 B.C. to 1400 B.C.). For the first time in modern history, the body of one of the great pharaohs was found in situ, inside his beautiful quartzite sarcophagus. But more astonishing than this was the presence in the main chamber of a second mummy laid to rest on top of a wooden boat, and twelve other mummies buried in two side chambers of the tomb—nine in one and three in the other.

Loret at first thought that these 12 bodies were private people of a later period who had chosen to share the king's final resting place. But on closer examination he discovered that at least nine of the fourteen bodies were kings: Tuthmosis IV, son of Amenhotep II; Amenhotep III, grandson of the tomb owner and father of the heretic king Akhenaton; Merenptah, son of Ramses the Great; and six kings of the 20th dynasty (Siptah and five kings named Ramses). When Howard Carter became chief inspector of antiquities at Qurna, he had the nine kings moved to the Cairo Museum, where they joined the previously discovered members of the New Kingdom royal line. The three bodies in the more northerly side room have been, and continue to be, the subject of intense debate. One, nicknamed the Elder Lady, is thought to be the body of Queen Tiye, wife of Amenhotep III and mother of Akhenaton. The second is a young man, and the gender of the third is uncertain, and has recently been at the center of a much publicized controversy.

BURIAL CHAMBER OF AMENHOTEP II
Valley of the Kings, Tomb of Amenhotep II
Excavations of the Egyptian Antiquities
  Service (Victor Loret), 1898–99

1898: The Gate of the Horse

Painted sandstone
Height 138 cm
Dynasty 11, reign of Mentuhotep II
Deir el-Bahri, mortuary temple of
  Mentuhotep II
Excavations of the Egyptian Antiquities
  Service (Howard Carter), 1900

THE DISCOVERY OF THIS POWERFUL STATUE OF NEBHEPETRE Mentuhotep (circa 2010 B.C. to 1960 B.C.) was made in 1898 by Howard Carter. Nebhepetre Mentuhotep was the fifth king of the 11th dynasty, which ruled southern Egypt from Thebes, jockeying for power with another royal line based at Herakleopolis. This warrior king brought the civil wars that had been raging for a century to an end, reuniting the Two Lands under the Theban banner. His ancestors had built their tombs in the Theban area, and Mentuhotep II chose a secluded bay of cliffs, now known as Deir el-Bahri, for his mortuary monument.

This statue was the first of Carter's great discoveries, and was made by accident. At the time, Carter, who had come to Egypt as an artist but stayed as an archaeologist, was working for a British organization called the Egypt Exploration Fund at Deir el-Bahri, most famous for the funerary temple of the female king Hatshepsut that dominates the site. One rainy November evening, Carter was on his way home when his horse's leg broke through the sodden ground into a small hole. Carter peered in and saw stonework. He was not able to explore this tantalizing trace for two years, until he had been appointed inspector general of antiquities for Upper Egypt. The hole, which he nicknamed the Bab el-Hosan, "Gate of the Horse," led to an intact chamber. Expecting great things—perhaps even a royal burial, since the chamber was clearly associated with the mortuary temple of Nebhepetre Mentuhotep—Carter prepared for the opening of the chamber with great pomp, even going so far as to invite important dignitaries. The results were disappointing by the standards of those days (although most of today's archaeologists would consider this a great find): Inside the chamber was this statue, wrapped in linen; an empty coffin; some wooden boats; and some pots.

The king, whose skin is black to associate him with the color of fertile earth (he is represented in many other depictions with the traditional reddish-yellow skin of the male Egyptian) wears the Red Crown, symbol of his authority over the territory of Lower Egypt. A final conclusion has not yet been reached about the purpose of this clearly symbolic burial; it may be related in some way with his Sed festival. This festival was in part a ceremony of rejuvenation (thus the black skin), and the reinstallation of the king as ruler of each of the Two Lands was an important event enacted during the ceremonies.

Animals have been responsible for several other great Egyptological discoveries. In 1900 the donkey of an antiquities guard at Alexandria stumbled across the Roman catacombs of Kom el-Shuqafa, and animals have played an important role in two of my own excavations, the Tombs of the Pyramid Builders (page 157) and the Valley of the Golden Mummies (page 180).

1899: Sacrificial Victims

ABYDOS WAS THE UNFORTUNATE TARGET OF FOUR YEARS OF RATHER
ABYDOS WAS THE UNFORTUNATE TARGET OF FOUR YEARS OF RATHER unscientific excavations by Frenchman Emile-Clément Amélineau, who simultaneously discovered and damaged the tombs of the 1st and 2nd dynasty kings at the Umm el-Qa'ab. His main interest was collecting salable antiquities, and he plowed through the site like a whirlwind, working at an alarming rate of speed. Rumor has it that he deliberately smashed pottery and stamped stone vases to bits, and even shattered several priceless ebony tablets inscribed with the names of the first kings of Egypt. But he did shed the first significant light on this previously unknown era.

Surrounding both the tombs of the 1st dynasty kings and their corresponding mortuary complexes were rows of smaller graves (more than 300 in one case) containing the bodies of royal retainers. Amélineau found the stela shown here in association with one of these subsidiary burials. The woman buried in the grave marked by this stone must have served the king during his lifetime, and may have been sacrificed at the time of his death in order to accompany her master into the afterlife.

Petrie was both fascinated by the site itself and outraged at its treatment by Amélineau. In 1899 he took it upon himself to open new excavations at the Umm el-Qa'ab, hoping to salvage some information from what had been left behind. He succeeded famously, and provided the scientific community with vast amounts of important information about the kings of this key period in Egyptian history.

By all accounts, Petrie was not an easy man to work with. He was puritanical and had no interest in creature comforts: He lived happily in a modest tent or abandoned tomb, ate whatever came to hand—usually out of a can—and expected everyone else to do the same. But the results of his work were spectacular by the standards of his time, both in terms of objects found and information recovered, and his publication record was exceptional.

ABYDOS SUBSIDIARY STELE
Limestone
Height 31 cm
Early Dynastic Period, Dynasty 1
Excavations of E. Amélineau, 1896

ANTHROPOID COFFIN

Cartonnage
Height 150 cm
Third Intermediate Period,
 reign of Osorkon I
Thebes, Valley of the Kings
Excavations of Howard Carter, 1901

THE EARLIEST EXAMPLES OF EGYPTIAN COFFINS ARE EITHER SQUARE OR rectangular, depending on whether the body was curled in a fetal position (seen in the earlier periods) or laid out straight (standard position by the middle of the Old Kingdom). During the Old Kingdom, a layer of plaster was often applied to the outside of the mummy and then modeled and painted as a likeness of the deceased. This is thought to have ensured that the person would be recognized in the afterlife, and also to have served as an alternative image in case the body was destroyed. In the late Old Kingdom, separate masks that fit over the head of the mummy began to appear; these were made of linen soaked with plaster (cartonnage) and then painted, again as an idealized image of the deceased. By the early Middle Kingdom, the faces of most mummies were covered by these masks. At the outset of this period, a new form of sarcophagus appeared. This was the anthropoid, mummiform coffin, which is first found in the tomb of one of Nebhepetre Mentuhotep's queens. At first, the coffin was painted white in imitation of the mummy bandages themselves, with only the head decorated to resemble the living person. As time passed, the coffins themselves took on various types of decoration, the most elaborate being covered with gold foil.

Howard Carter discovered this elegant cartonnage coffin on January 26, 1901, during his tenure as chief inspector of antiquities for the Theban area. It lay within a pit in the Valley of the Kings that was already known to the local reis. Carter decided that rather than waiting for tomb robbers to beat him to the still unopened pit, he would investigate it himself. The work took two days. A closed door lay beneath more than 5 meters (about 16 feet) of "rubbish." Beyond it lay a chamber containing three wooden coffins bedecked with wreaths of flowers. The elegant anthropoid coffin of Lady Tjentkerersherit (Lady Tjentkerer the Younger), its fresh, youthful face wearing a lifelike expression, lay nested inside a rough wooden outer coffin. Her headdress bears a winged scarab, image of Khepri, god of the sunrise and thus a powerful symbol of rebirth. The bottom of the coffin bears an image of the cow of Hathor, another sign of eternal resurrection.

The mummy itself was inside, wrapped in fine linen but with no other funerary objects except a pair of red leather braces, the ends stamped with a yellow inscription bearing the cartouches of Osorkon I. This king ruled during the Third Intermediate period, when Libyan princes reigned in the delta, sharing power with the High Priests of Amon at Thebes. The two ruling houses coexisted peacefully for the most part, even intermarrying from time to time. We do not know who Tjentkerersherit was, except that she must have been related in some way to Osorkon I.

ANTHROPOID COFFIN
Cartonnage
Length 150 cm
Third Intermediate Period, Dynasty 22
Thebes, Valley of the Kings
Excavation of Howard Carter, 1901

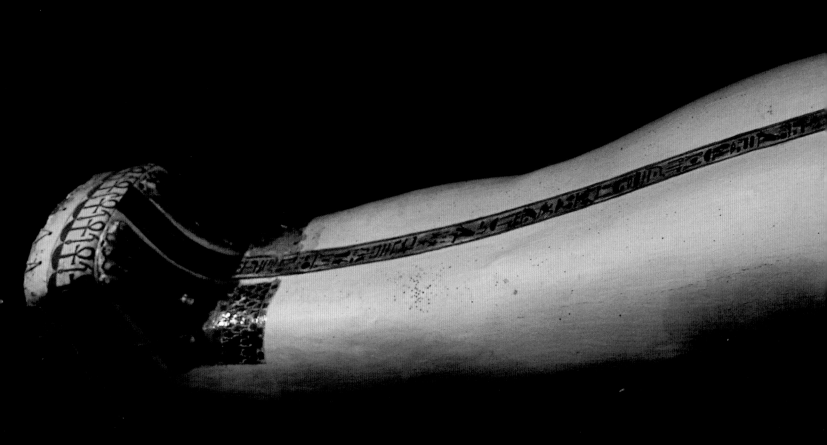

NAOPHOROUS STATUE OF SEBTY
Quartzite
Height 32 cm
Dynasty 18, reign of Amenhotep III
Karnak, Court of the Cachette
Excavations of the Egyptian Antiquities
  Service, (Georges Legrain), 1903–05

TO THE DELIGHT AND RELIEF OF MANY EGYPTOLOGISTS, GASTON MASPERO had returned to Cairo in 1899 to resume his post as director of the Antiquities Service. That October a number of columns in the great hypostyle hall built by Seti I and Ramses II at the great Amon Temple of Karnak collapsed. Maspero asked a French architect, Georges Legrain, to oversee their restoration, ordering Legrain to extract as much information as possible and to uncover any interesting objects that might be hidden there. Legrain made a number of important finds, and in 1903 his workmen hit pay dirt—the largest cache of major artifacts found in Egypt.

This find was made in the winter, when the Nile and the water table were high, and the workers had to squelch through the mud to extract the statues, stelae, and bronzes that began to flow from their ancient hiding place. Over the course of two years of work, 751 statues and statue fragments, 17,000 bronzes, and many other pieces were recovered. Finally, Legrain was forced to stop work at the site because the high water table made further excavations impossible. The majority of the finds were probably votive pieces set up at the temple and then collected and given ritual burial by priests in the Ptolemaic period. Spanning 3,000 years, these artifacts provide a unique record of private and royal votive activity over the course of Egyptian history.

When I became head of the Supreme Council of Antiquities I set up the Department of Returning Stolen Antiquities and wrote a letter addressed to all the institutions and scholars around the world having a connection with Egyptology. Since 1983 Egyptian antiquities law had forbidden artifacts to leave the country without government permission. In my letter I asked for the return of any objects that fit this description and announced that any institutions that had in their collections artifacts that had left the country illegally, especially those that had crossed the border after the UNESCO convention in 1972, would no longer be granted the right of scientific cooperation with Egypt. In addition, individuals dealing in stolen artifacts would be prosecuted. The Department of Returning Stolen Antiquities has been working to compile a list of artifacts considered stolen, trying to trace them and get them back, and trying to pursue leads on any other black-market activities.

This quartzite statue of a priest of Montu named Sebty had disappeared from a storeroom at Karnak many years ago. It was seized in Holland and brought back to Egypt on May 17, 2002. The now headless statue dates from the time of Amenhotep III (circa 1390 B.C. to 1353 B.C.). Montu was the patron god of war; his principal cult was practiced at Armant, although he was also worshiped in Thebes. Sebty is dressed for a festival in a billowing linen dress. In front of him he holds a naos, within which is depicted Montu in the form of a falcon. The text on the statue indicates that the image was dedicated to Sebty by his son, Amenemipet, also a high priest of Montu.

IN THE LATE 700S B.C., EGYPT WAS CONQUERED BY A FOREIGN POWER, THE Kushite dynasty from Nubia, and for the first time in its history, became part of someone else's empire. Several decades later, the Assyrian empire rising to the north invaded Egypt twice, sacked Thebes, and drove the Nubians back to their homeland. The Assyrians were supported by a native dynasty, presumed to be of Libyan origin, based in the delta. Psammetik I (664 B.C. to 610 B.C.) soon claimed independence from the overextended Assyrians and reunited the country under the banner of the Saite 26th dynasty.

This small sphinx, which probably once stood inside Karnak Temple, illustrates the deliberately archaizing royal art of the Saite period. Although Psammetik I ruled for 54 years, most Saite art dates from the kings who succeeded him; this is the only clearly identified three-dimensional image we have of him that retains its head. The face is serene, the mouth a thin, expressionless line. The eyes are the only unusual feature: They are almond shaped and slope downward slightly at the corners. The name of the king is inscribed on the chest: "Son of Re, Psametik, beloved of Amon-re."

SPHINX OF PSAMMETIK

Calcite
Height 47 cm/43.5 cm; Width 62 cm
Dynasty 26, reign of Psammetik I,
   around 650 B.C.
Karnak, Court of the Cachette
Excavations of the Egyptian Antiquities
   Service (George Legrain), 1903-05

STATUETTE OF KHUFU
Ivory
Height 7.5 cm
Abydos, Temple of Khentiamentiu
Dynasty 4, Reign of Khufu
Excavations of Petrie, 1903

1903: The Great Pyramid Builder

THIS TINY STATUETTE, THE ONLY SECURELY ATTRIBUTED IMAGE OF THE builder of the Great Pyramid, is one of my favorite objects in the collection of the Cairo Museum. It was found in 1903 by Petrie, who was continuing his work at Abydos in an area close to the edge of the floodplain where the temple to the mortuary god Khenti-imentiu once stood.

Petrie's workmen were digging in a room connected with this temple when they came across a headless statuette of ivory, which they brought to show the great Egyptologist. Recognizing the name of Khufu, one of the greatest kings in history, inscribed on the base, Petrie was immediately aware of the importance of this find. The break across the neck was clearly fresh, probably made by the pickax of one of the workmen, so Petrie set a border around the area where it had been found. He then sent several workmen to the nearest large town to buy every sieve they could find and set his crew to scrutinizing every bit of sand in the area, looking for the head. Three weeks later, a shout went up—it had been found!

The repaired statuette shows Khufu holding a flail and wearing the Red Crown of Lower Egypt. This king ruled for more than 32 years and built a monument that still stands as one of humankind's greatest achievements. I believe that this statuette may be a copy of an Old Kingdom original and may date from the 26th dynasty (664 B.C. to 525 B.C.), when the cult of this great monarch was revived.

The man who found the head was the grandfather of one of the native excavators who trained me in fieldwork, Reis Doctoor. The family of this man, and many of the men who worked with Petrie, were from a village in Upper Egypt named Quft. Petrie trained these men well, and their descendents have been in great demand as excavation supervisors and conservation experts ever since.

statuette in 1911 at the site of Tell el-Amarna, the city of the heretic king Akhenaton. This king is probably best known today as the husband of the beautiful Nefertiti and the likely father of Tutankhamun. Leaving Thebes after several years as king, Akhenaton, who took the Egyptian throne as Amenhotep IV, renounced the worship of all gods but one, the sun disk (the Aten), and changed his name. He set up a new capital at Amarna, which he called Akhetaten, Horizon of the Aten, and built temples there dedicated to his god. Stelae from the site show him with his queen, Nefertiti, and their daughters (six in all), bathing in the rays of the sun disk. In fact, it seems that he and Nefertiti were themselves worshiped with the Aten, which he refers to as "my father" and which may in reality have been identified with his human father, Amenhotep III.

This statue, in the radical new exaggerated style characteristic of his reign, represents the king himself in the blue "war helmet," a crown connected with his coronation, making offerings to the Aten. Akhenaton is shown with a slightly long face, wide hips, and swollen belly, probably a fairly realistic portrayal of his actual appearance. Theories abound as to why Akhenaton is not shown with the idealized face and body typical of earlier royal images; the two most current hypotheses are that he suffered from a genetic disorder called Marfan's syndrome or that the style of his art was related to his religious revolution. There is also a great deal of debate about whether Akhenaton ruled alongside his father, Amenhotep III, as a co-regent or whether they ruled consecutively.

At some point in his reign, Akhenaton went even further and closed the temples of all gods other than the Aten, ordering that their names, especially that of Amon, be removed from all monuments. Soon after his death, however, the priests of Amon regained power. Akhetaten was abandoned, and Akhenaton's name, along with the names of his successors, was wiped from history.

STATUE OF AMENEMOPE
Painted limestone
Height 26 cm
Dynasty 19 to 20
Deir el-Medineh, Temple of Hathor
Excavations of Émile Baraize, 1912
Egyptian Museum

1912: Deir el-Medineh

EMILE BARAIZE (1874–1952) FOUND THIS NAOPHOROUS STATUE OF Amenemope at the workmen's village at Deir el-Medineh in 1912. Baraize, who first came to Egypt as a technical draftsman for the Egyptian railways, worked primarily on reconstruction and restoration for the Antiquities Service. Perhaps his most significant work was at Giza, where he carried out clearance and repair work on the Sphinx.

The inhabitants of Deir el-Medineh gave a great deal of attention to religion, and several large temples and a number of smaller chapels were associated with the village. To the north of the village Seti I built a large chapel to Hathor, goddess of music and love and daughter-wife of Amon-Re, where she was worshiped by the workmen and their families. The villagers acted as their own priests and had personal relationships with their gods.

In the Ptolemaic period a great temple to Hathor was built on the same site as the earlier Hathor chapel, and it was within this precinct that Amenemope's statue was found. Baraize's work was focused on clearance and reconstruction, but, as is common in these cases, even today, many interesting objects were found by the excavators. The original publication of this object is very sketchy, only listing it within the catalogue of finds with no other specific information. The statue, which is similar in iconography to the image of Sebty (page 71), shows Amenemope, an artisan who lived at Deir el-Medineh, wearing the garments of a high official, a curled wig, and a ceremonial beard. Like Sebty, he is offering a naos, in this case with the head of a falcon on top. This votive image was dedicated by Amenemope's son Qenherkhepeshef.

1930: The Treasures of Tutankhamun

complete without the mask of Tutankhamun, without a doubt the most famous artifact in the collections. It is known around the world, and has been copied on T-shirts, jewelry, in logos, and everywhere else one could imagine. It, together with the Giza pyramids, the Great Sphinx, and mummies, has come to symbolize Egypt's ancient past.

The story of the discovery of Tutankhamun's tomb is one of the best-known and oft-told stories in the history of Egyptian archaeology. I myself heard it from an eyewitness, a man named Sheikh Ali, whom I met when I was a young archaeologist first starting out and he was a man of 70. Sheikh Ali was a member of the Abd al-Rassoul family, discoverers of the Deir el-Bahri cache of royal mummies, and he, like many of the members of the family, was part of the team hired by the central figure in this tale, Howard Carter. In 1922, Carter, under the sponsorship of Lord Carnarvon, had been excavating in the Valley of the Kings for a number of seasons, looking for the tomb of Tutankhamun. The name of this king had appeared on scattered artifacts and statues, but little was known about him. He was not included in any of the ancient king lists, and his mummy had not been present in either of the royal caches. Thus Carter hoped that the tomb of this elusive pharaoh might still be intact, and had picked up on several clues that convinced him that it was in the royal valley. By the end of the previous season, which like the others had produced nothing substantial in the way of results, Carnarvon had decided to give up. He called Carter to his home in England and told him that the search was over. But Carter was not ready to quit and offered to pay for the next season out of his own pocket. Carnarvon, impressed at his dedication, relented and agreed to fund several more months of work.

Gold and semiprecious stones
Height 9 cm; Width 10.5 cm
Dynasty 18, reign of Tutankhamun
Valley of the Kings, tomb of Tutankhamun
Carter-Carnarvon excavations, 1922–30

CARTER ARRIVED IN THE VALLEY OF THE KINGS IN LATE FALL OF 1922, AND work began immediately. Having exhausted all the other possibilities, he told his team to begin exploring an area near the entrance to the valley which was covered by the remains of workmen's huts dating to the 20th dynasty. Carter told his workers to record them and then clear them away. On the second day of the dig, a water boy brushed away some sand so that he could set down his jars and uncovered a step of limestone, which led to a stairway just below the surface.

Carter had his team clear the stairway, which led down beneath the bedrock to a blocked doorway, plastered and stamped with the seals of the ancient necropolis police. Halting the work, he set a guard on the site and sent a telegram to Carnarvon telling him to return to Egypt from England. Upon the nobleman's arrival, the debris in front of the doorway was cleared, and the name of Tutankhamun was revealed for the first time. Beyond this wall lay a rubble-filled corridor, and then a second blocked doorway, also stamped with the necropolis seals. Beyond the second doorway lay four rooms filled with glittering gold and masterpiece after masterpiece of Egyptian art. Over the next decade, a wealth of fabulous objects poured from the chambers of the tomb.

This beautiful jewel bears the throne name of Tutankhamun: Nebkheperure. The craftsman has cleverly used the hieroglyphic elements of the royal name to create a work of both great beauty and significance. The winged scarab beetle, hieroglyph for *kheper*, meaning "to happen, to become," is in the center; this insect was an important symbol of creation. Below the beetle are three strokes which make the kheper sign plural, and a basket, the sign for *neb*, "Lord."

The tomb of Tutankhamun contained 35 wooden models of boats (OVER-LEAF), which were stored with his equipment for the symbolic transportation of the king and the sun god through the sky of the underworld. These models provide a great deal of information about the various types of boats used in ancient Egypt. Seen here are examples with masts for sails, steering paddles, and single- or double-storied cabins, decorated with colored geometric motifs. Some have stairs, and others are provided with kiosks for the lookout or for the captain.

These boats were among objects belonging to Tutankhamun's tomb that were stored in the basement of the Cairo Museum and had never been seen by either scholars or the public.

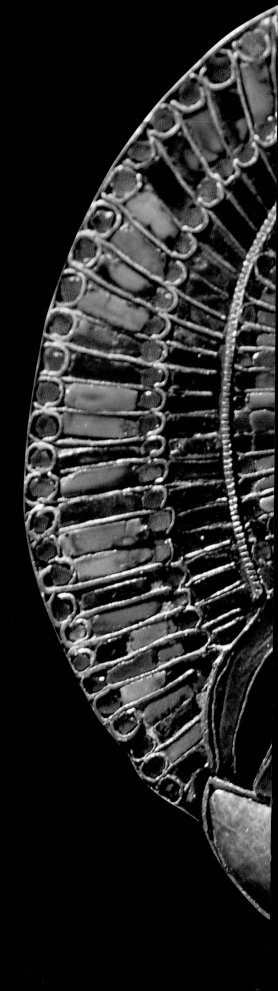

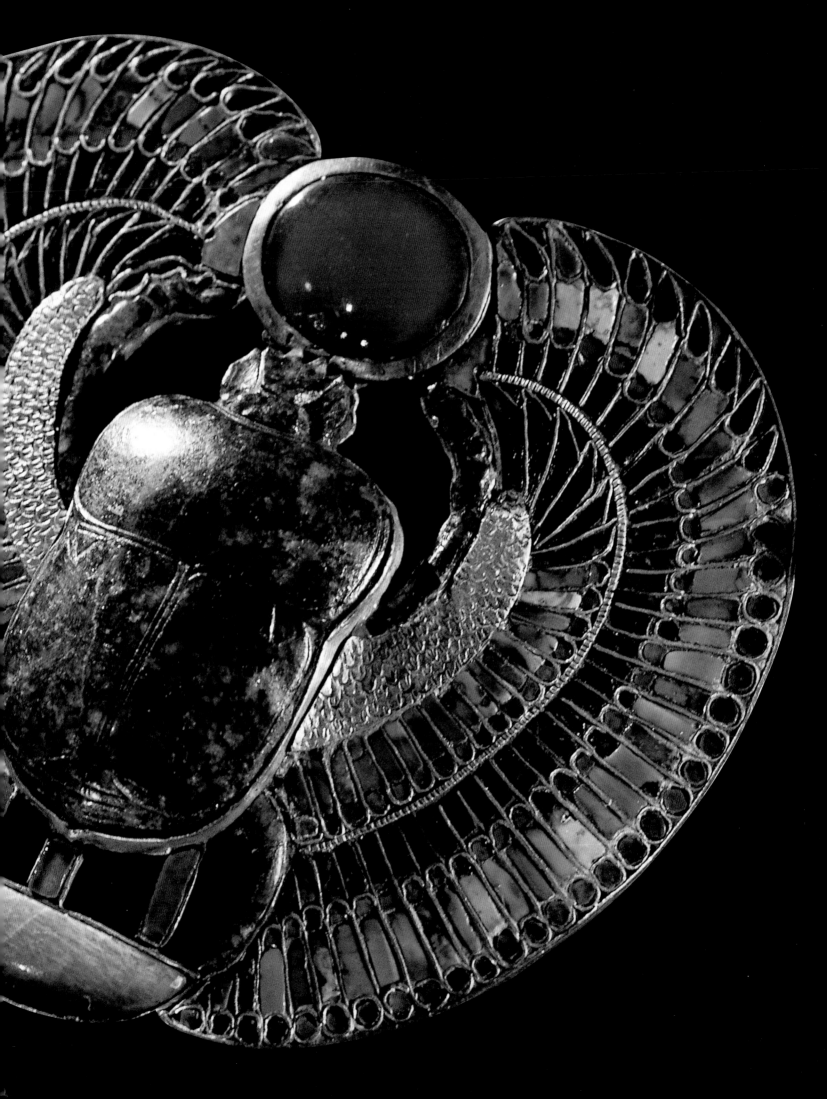

FOUR MODEL BOATS
Wood
Left (papyrus model): 124 cm; model with paddle
 and mast: 114 cm; model with double-storied
 cabin 109 cm; model with smaller cabin 70 cm
Dynasty 18, reign of Tutankhamun
Valley of the Kings, tomb of Tutankhamun
Carter-Carnarvon excavations, 1922–30

were important ones for the future of Egyptology in Egypt. Drawn by the spectacular nature of the finds and by the furor in the foreign press, the upper classes of Egypt became more interested in their ancient past. Tourists flocked to Egypt to see the tomb. However, all of this was not necessarily good news for Carter and Carnarvon. Problems were created right at the beginning when Carter, in an attempt to limit access to the tomb, gave exclusive rights to the Tutankhamun story to the London *Times*. The rest of the press corps, and especially the native Egyptian press, felt wrongly excluded. Carter, feeling that the discovery belonged to Britain, was less than hospitable to his erstwhile colleagues in the Antiquities Service. He did not even invite Pierre Lacau, then head of the Service, to the official opening of the tomb. This sort of behavior, coupled with Carter's and Carnarvon's insistence that they had a right to half of the objects found in the tomb, led to many difficulties. Carter was even locked out of the tomb until he would sign a paper agreeing that the Egyptian government had a right to keep the entire Tutankhamun collection in Egypt. It is believed by many scholars that Carter did, in fact, smuggle several pieces out of the tomb.

Nonetheless, Carter assembled an excellent team to help record, conserve, and transport the objects in the tomb. This piece, like most of the headrests found in Tutankhamun's tomb, was found in the Annexe, a rectangular chamber to the west of the antechamber that contained vessels for food, wine, oil, and unguents, and also served to hold the overflow of furniture and funerary figurines from other chambers. This headrest is unusual, as it is designed to fold. We know from the many representations of hunting found on objects within the tomb that the young king was a keen sportsman, and a folding bed found in the tomb is thought to have been used on hunting expeditions. This headrest might thus have been used for overnight trips to the desert, where wild game was plentiful. It is made of ivory tinted in shades of red, green, black, and yellow. The flexible pillow is formed of multicolored ivory beads. The tops of the pillow terminals are decorated with lotus flowers (which carry connotations of sexuality and fertility), and the undersides are carved with heads of Bes, a household god. The legs are hinged with gold, and end in ducks' heads. One of Tutankhamun's names, Nebkheperure, is carved onto one of the legs.

CHARIOT FITTING
Gold
Height 9.5 cm; Width 19.5 cm
Dynasty 18, reign of Tutankhamun
Thebes, Valley of the Kings, tomb
  of Tutankhamun
Carter-Carnarvon excavations, 1922–30

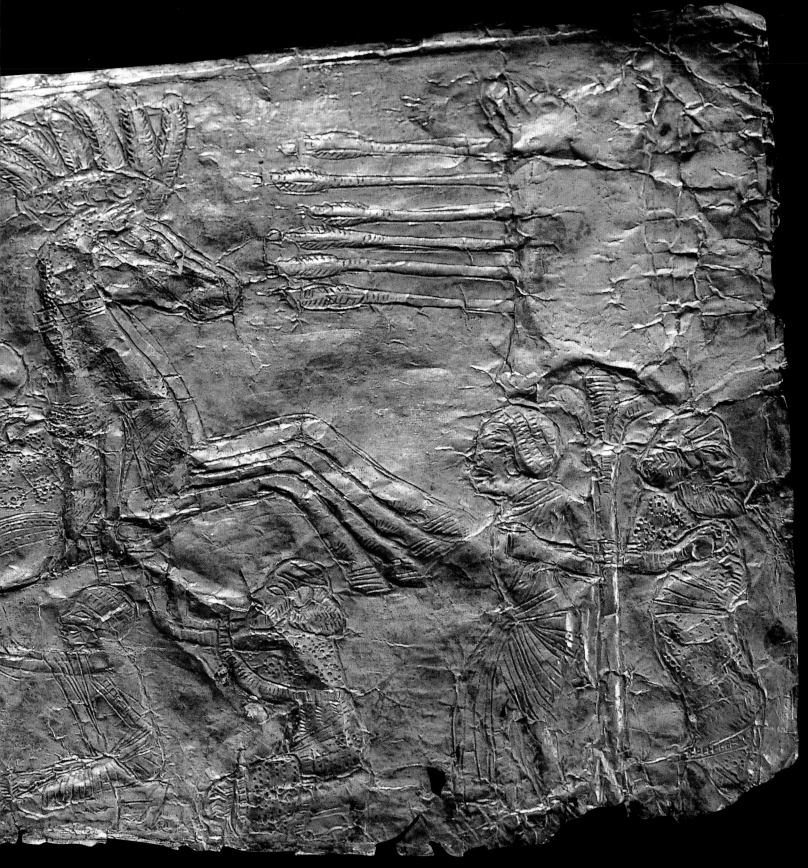

THE TOMB OF TUTANKHAMUN YIELDED OVER 5,000 ARTIFACTS. THEY TELL the story of a young king who came to the throne as a child and died before the age of twenty. He was most likely the son of the "heretic" pharaoh Akhenaten by a minor wife named Kiya; some have speculated that Akhenaten's chief queen, Nefertiti, had his mother killed out of jealousy, since she bore only daughters to her royal husband. Tutankhamun, born Tutankhaten, was married to one of Nefertiti's daughters, his half-sister Ankhsenpaaten. At some point after he came to the throne, the still-powerful priests of Amun either persuaded or forced the young royal couple to return to the old religion, and changed their names to Tutankhamun and Akhsenamun.

Despite his return to the old state religion, Tutankhamun belonged to an era that was considered an affront to Egyptian sensibilities, and was soon officially wiped from the history books. His small, hastily completed tomb was forgotten and buried under the debris from a later royal burial. Thus the mummy of the boy king and the furnishings that he took with him into the afterlife were preserved for posterity.

Assurances of fertility and rebirth were vital to the successful Afterlife of the ancient Egyptian. This charming object is both aesthetically pleasing and magically effective–by showing the moment when this baby bird emerges from its shell, the artist symbolically represents and thus helps to ensure the rebirth of the piece's owner. The young duckling is carved out of painted wood; its tongue is of stained ivory.

1925: The Tomb of Hetepheres

THE OBJECTS HERE FORM PART OF A HIDDEN BURIAL DISCOVERED BY A team working for American archaeologist George Reisner. In February 1925, while Reisner was in the United States, a member of his team, Egyptian Egyptologist Mohamadin Ibrahim, was setting up a tripod to the east of the Great Pyramid. One of the legs sank into a depression in the sand, and when he investigated, he found a limestone slab that covered the top of a stairway. Reisner returned to Egypt immediately, and the team found that the stairway led to a vertical shaft about 27 meters (91 feet) deep. Mixed with the fill were sealings, bits of mud stamped with official seals, from Khufu's mortuary workshop, and at the bottom was a chamber containing the sarcophagus of Queen Hetepheres, mother of Khufu, along with many items of funerary furniture. Excavation of this tomb took ten years.

This rich tomb is one of the mysteries of Egyptian archaeology. The furniture was carelessly placed and, although the queen's canopic equipment was present, her great alabaster sarcophagus was empty. I believe that Hetepheres was originally buried in one of the small pyramids east of the Great Pyramid, which were built for the queens of Khufu. It is likely that her burial was vandalized during the First Intermediate period and that priests loyal to Khufu moved what remained of his mother's burial into the shaft where it was found to save it further destruction.

FUNERARY FURNITURE OF HETEPHERES
Dynasty 4, reign of Sneferu and Khufu
Giza, Tomb of Hetepheres
Excavations of George Reisner, 1925

1928–30: The Alabaster Panel of Rawer

SELIM HASSAN, WHO STUDIED FIRST WITH AHMED KAMAL AND LATER IN Paris, began his career as an excavator in 1928, working with the German archaeologist Hermann Junker at Giza. A year later he was leading his own team from Cairo University, which carried out important work at both Giza and Saqqara for the next ten years. This beautiful and unique alabaster stela was found during Hassan's 1929–30 season in the tomb of a 5th dynasty official named Rawer. This is one of the largest private tombs known from the Old Kingdom. It lies in the cemetery south of Khafre's causeway. It is not in the usual form of a rectangular mastaba, but instead is a complex of irregular, seemingly randomly placed chambers.

In contrast to the typical number of *serdabs*—enclosed chambers in which statues were hidden—or niches found in such tombs (rarely more than five), Rawer's tomb has twenty-five serdabs and twenty niches. Hassan estimated that there were once more than a hundred statues and statuettes of Rawer contained in the tomb. This man, who evidently commanded unusual wealth, may have been connected with the royal family in some way through his mother's blood: Her name, like that of Khufu's mother, was Hetepheres. Rawer bore many titles, some priestly, some administrative, and some connected with the person of the king. Perhaps the most interesting of his titles were Master of the Secrets of the Toilet House and Hairdresser of the King. The stela we see here was set into the back of a mud-brick niche, approached by a series of three steps.

FUNERARY STELA
Limestone
Height 20 cm; Width 30 cm
Roman period (second to third century A.D.)
Kom Abu Billo (Terenuthis)
University of Michigan excavations, 1935

1935: Sailing to Eternity

MORE THAN 200 FUNERARY STELAE WERE DISCOVERED DURING EXCAVATIONS carried out by the University of Michigan in 1935 in the southeast corner of Kom Abu Billo, which is the modern name of the necropolis of the ancient city of Terenuthis (El-Tarana) on the western edge of the delta (63 kilometers [40 miles] northwest of Cairo). Most of the group is part of the collections of the Kelsey Museum at the University of Michigan. The remainder, including this piece, were kept in the Cairo Museum, stored in the basement, where we found them while collecting objects for the Hidden Treasures exhibit. This stela shows the deceased, a young boy, reclining in a boat. He wears a robe and holds the steering oar with his right hand; his left hand is raised in an attitude of adoration. The style of the stela and the clothing of the dead boy are entirely classical; the journey of the soul across the River Styx to the land of the dead is also a Greek concept. The stela itself, and its placement in the tomb, blends Greek and Egyptian beliefs about the afterlife.

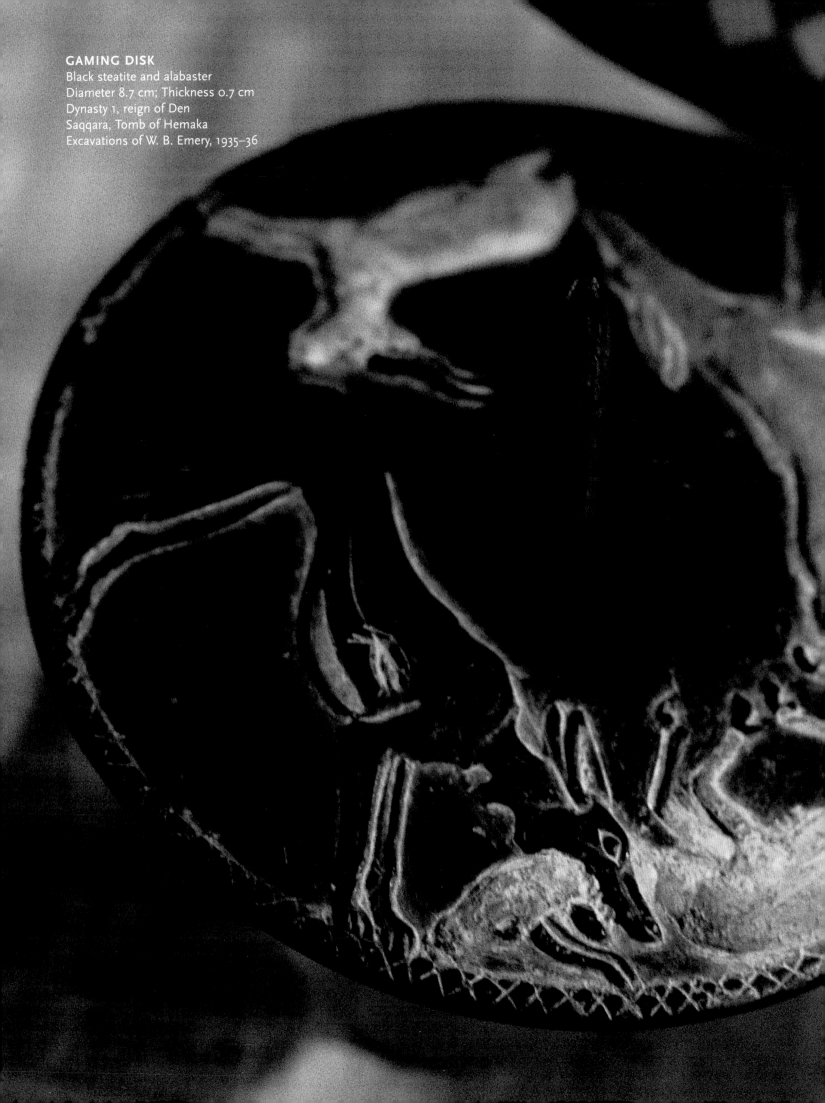

GAMING DISK
Black steatite and alabaster
Diameter 8.7 cm; Thickness 0.7 cm
Dynasty 1, reign of Den
Saqqara, Tomb of Hemaka
Excavations of W. B. Emery, 1935–36

1936: Tombs of the Nobles at Saqqara

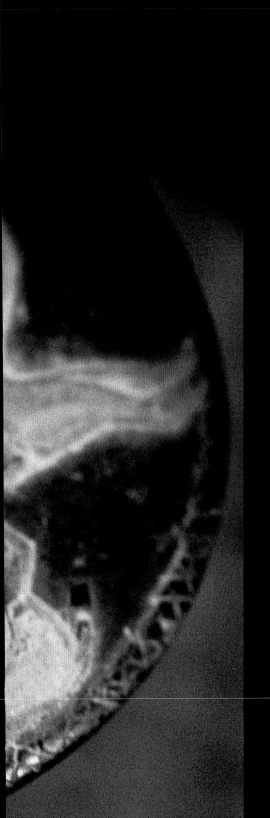

IN 1935 WALTER BRYAN EMERY, WHO HAD A LONG AND DISTINGUISHED career as both a professor at the University of London and a field archaeologist in Egypt, set out to excavate a series of enormous mud-brick mastabas at Saqqara. These had been built during the 1st and 2nd dynasties and were extremely elaborate, with massive walls decorated with complex niches once plastered and painted to imitate reed matting. Like their counterparts at Abydos, some of these were surrounded by subsidiary burials; some were also surrounded by the horned skulls of cattle, evidently a sign of status and wealth.

The excavation of these tombs opened a new debate about the location of the royal tombs of the 1st dynasty. Emery, impressed by the sheer size of the Saqqara mastabas, argued that these were the true burials of the great kings, and that the structures at Abydos were cenotaphs, ritual tombs in which no royal burial had ever been made. Royally inscribed material, especially sealings and small labels (pages 158–59), was found at both sites, as were texts naming private people; thus both sets of tombs were legitimate candidates for the royal tombs of this dynasty. In the end, it was their size and the elaborateness of their architecture that convinced Emery that the Saqqara tombs were the principal burials of these kings.

More recently, another great British Egyptologist, Barry Kemp, has convincingly argued that the Abydos tombs were for the kings themselves, while the Saqqara tombs were built for high officials. He points out that, although the Saqqara tombs themselves are larger, if the Abydos tomb for each king and its associated mortuary complex are added together, they cover significantly more area than the Saqqara mastabas alone. It is also possible, based on the inscribed material found at each site, to attribute the Saqqara mastabas to high officials; there is no question that the Abydos tombs, each of which was once fronted by a pair of large stelae bearing the royal name, belonged to the kings themselves.

Emery found the disk illustrated here at Saqqara, in a tomb that the excavator attributed to King Den. More recent scholarship concluded that the owner was a high official named Hemaka, who seems to have served as treasurer and possibly also acted as vizier. The disk was found in a wooden box along with a number of other disks of various materials. The purpose of these objects is unknown: Emery suggested that they were placed on sticks and then spun, like modern tops.

1939–40: The Gold of Tanis

THIS SPECTACULAR SILVER COFFIN COMES FROM ONE OF A GROUP OF royal tombs discovered in 1939 by Pierre Montet (1885–1966), a French Egyptologist trained by Victor Loret. Until recently, these fabulous finds have been relatively neglected in favor of the far better known treasures of Tutankhamun. The timing of their discovery, in an era when the world had far graver concerns than the tombs of long-dead kings, was unfortunate. In addition, the period in which these pharaohs lived, the Third Intermediate period, was neither as well known nor considered as interesting as the New Kingdom.

Montet had been excavating at Tanis in the eastern delta for ten years, uncovering traces of a huge temple complex dedicated to Amon that had first been explored by Mariette and later by Petrie. This temple was built by Psusennes I of the 21st dynasty and contained many inscribed artifacts dating to various earlier pharaohs, such as Khufu and Khafre from the Old Kingdom and Senwosret I from the Middle Kingdom. By far the most common royal name found on these monuments is Ramses II. However, none of the buildings on the site predate Psusennes I, so it is likely that this king brought in the earlier inscribed material from nearby sites to reuse as building stone.

The first royal tomb came to light in February 1939. It lay inside the Amon Temple's enclosure wall, under a small temple dedicated to the goddess Mut. The original superstructure of the tomb had vanished long ago and the tomb beneath had been forgotten. Entering the first burial through the roof of the antechamber, Montet found himself in the tomb of King Osorkon III, a Libyan prince who ruled Egypt during the 22nd dynasty. To his amazement, a second tomb lay near the first, and then another and another and another: There were a total of six royal tombs at the site. Most contained objects of gold and silver, and two were completely intact.

This beautiful sarcophagus was found in the tomb of Psusennes I, within the burial chamber. It lay nested inside two larger sarcophagi of granite, one of which dated to the reign of Merneptah of the 19th dynasty. It is of solid silver, the band around the king's forehead and the uraeus that surmounts his brow are made of gold, and its eyes are inlaid with glass paste. The king wears the long, curled beard of divinity and holds the crook and flail, symbols of royal power..

SARCOPHAGUS OF PSUSENNES I
Silver and gold
Height 185 cm
Tanis, Tomb of Psusennes I, crypt of
  Psusennes I
Third Intermediate period, reign of
  Psusennes I
Excavations of Pierre Montet, 1940

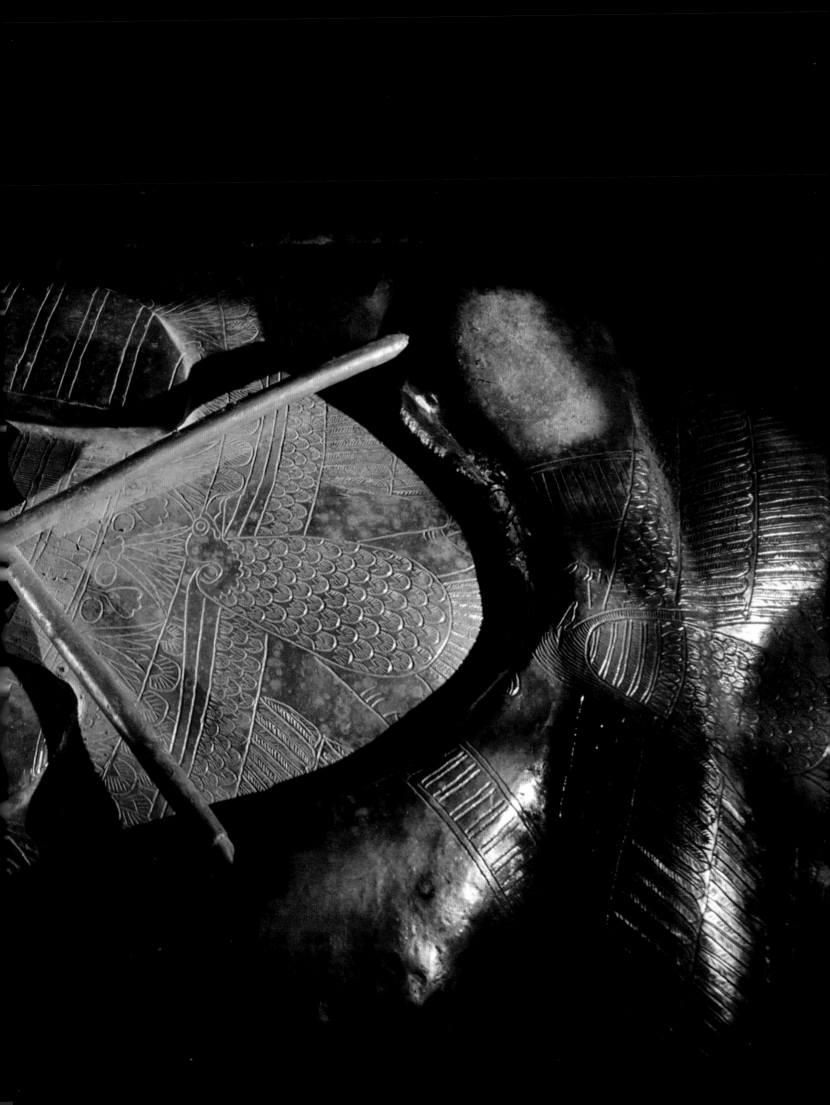

II. THE ERA OF INTERNATIONAL COOPERATION

1950 TO THE PRESENT

OLD KINGDOM STATUES, GIZA
Excavations of Abu Bakr, 1950

THE MIDDLE OF THE 20TH CENTURY MARKS AN IMPORTANT watershed in both Egyptological and Egyptian history. Egyptology led the way: In 1951 a bust of Ahmed Kamal was set up in the garden of the Cairo Museum. There were already many monuments and inscriptions to archaeologists in this garden, including the tomb of Auguste Mariette (who is actually buried in the garden), but Kamal was the first Egyptian to be honored in this way.

On the political front, Egyptian nationalism came to fruition in 1952 under Gamal Abdel Nasser, who led the coup that gave the Egyptians their independence.

The Antiquities Service had become more Egyptianized since the 1920s. But it was not until Egypt became fully independent that an Egyptian, Mustafa Amer, was appointed head of the Service. Since that time Egyptians have led the Service, and I am proud to be part of a group that includes distinguished Egyptologists such as Ahmed Khadry and Gamal Mokhtar. The Antiquities Service has undergone two major reorganizations since 1953. The first was in 1977, when the construction of the Aswan High Dam brought Nubian antiquities to the forefront of world attention. An extensive salvage campaign was launched, which included moving the temple of Ramses II at Abu Simbel to higher ground. To raise money for this campaign, an exhibit of objects from Tutankhamun's golden tomb was sent around the world. This raised Egypt's profile and created a great wave of enthusiasm for the pharaonic past both abroad and at home. The increased needs of the Antiquities Service led to a presidential decree replacing it with the larger, more complex Egyptian Antiquities Organization (EAO), with Gamal Mokhtar as its head. Increased funding and an international profile allowed new departments to be established and more staff to be hired.

In 1994 Minister of Culture Farouk Hosni decided that he wanted to be better informed about the activities of the EAO and to give its projects and departments greater independence. This resulted in another presidential decree that turned the Egyptian Antiquities Organization into the Supreme Council of Antiquities (SCA), with better financing and a number of new mandates. Abdel el-Halim nur ed-Din, who was a professor of language at Cairo University, served as the first secretary-general; the second was Gaballa Ali Gaballa, who is a professor of Egyptology at Cairo University. I am the third. The staff of the SCA now numbers about 30,000 people.

The past half-century has seen many improvements and refinements in archaeology around the

Reis Ibrahim el-Sherief, Mohammed Abdel Tawab, and (center) Abdel Moneim Abu Bakr in Aswan, 1963.

world, and archaeologists in Egypt are working hard to stay at the forefront of the field. This is not easy; several hundred years of colonialism have left us with many serious problems, including those of education and salary, which make it hard for us to find, train, and keep good people. But we now have many excellent young archaeologists working for the SCA, and they are being trained in the most advanced techniques available.

On the other side, our foreign colleagues are not yet required to learn Arabic as part of their advanced studies, although Egyptian scholars are all expected to learn at least English, French, and German. Thus, Egyptians are forced to publish in a foreign language to have any sort of international profile or audience, whereas our foreign colleagues can publish in their native tongues.

There have been, and will continue to be, some clashes of culture. Egypt is not a Western nation, and there are some issues that arise when two very different societies interact. Sometimes foreign archaeologists forget that they are guests in Egypt and become possessive of their concessions; many foreign archaeologists also continue to excavate, uncovering new material without publishing what they have already found. However, we have much more in common than we have dividing us. Relations between Egyptian and foreign archaeologists are generally excellent, and continue to develop in positive ways, as we all work together toward common goals.

The primary goal of every modern excavator is to recover as much knowledge as possible from

Kamal el Mallakh, discoverer of the Boat of Kufu

each site, and many new techniques and methods have been brought into the standard excavation repertoire. Every grain of sand is now sieved, and more comprehensive recovery methods are applied to all archaeological fill. It is now possible, for example, to collect tiny bits of pollen for bioarchaeological study or to analyze the clay from which a particular pot is made to see whether it was local or imported. The advent of carbon-14 dating has made it possible to get scientific confirmation or rejection of absolute dates (dates given in A.D./B.C. or B.C.E./C.E., rather than regnal dates). Noninvasive techniques for studying the past have also become more powerful: Mummies and skeletons can be analyzed with x-rays and CT scans, and sites can be partially mapped using remote sensing equipment.

Along with a preoccupation with methodology has come a greater concern for site conservation and preservation. This is a Sisyphean task. As the population of Egypt has boomed, construction of new houses and roads has impinged upon many ancient sites. Many of these sites are vast and/or remote; guards who are paid eighty pounds a month (the equivalent of a little more than ten dollars) and local authorities who are equally poorly paid have little incentive to do their jobs diligently and a great deal of incentive to take *baksheesh* (bribes) to look the other way. Inspectors all over the country have official backing to stop illegal construction of new houses on antiquities land but can do nothing in the face of powerful local headmen who are the real authorities in many places.

At least officially, though, the situation is improving somewhat. Building is still permitted on land that is under SCA supervision, but an archaeological team must be present any time ground is broken. Important finds made as a direct result of this law include a 26th dynasty tomb in Heliopolis and the enormous temple of Min at Akhmim, which is now being excavated. There is also an important new project under way by the SCA, in partnership with the Finnish Environmental

Institute, to map the legal boundaries of all the sites in Egypt, clarify their status, and work actively to protect them both from illegal encroachments and from legally sanctioned actions that would damage our cultural heritage.

Another major problem that we are facing is that with the building of the Aswan Dam and the spewing of uncontrolled sewage from the burgeoning population into the earth has come a dangerous rise in both the level and the salinity of the groundwater. In places such as Heliopolis and Luxor, standing water can be seen in many monuments, and many excavations, especially in the delta, are severely hampered by the high groundwater. In the 1980s Giza faced a similar problem; the Great Sphinx was in particular danger because of its location at the edge of the plateau. This problem was addressed by the installation of a new sewage system in the suburb that surrounds the site, which was successful on several fronts: The level of the groundwater was lowered, and in the process of making soundings and digging trenches for the laying of new pipe, parts of the settlement associated with the Giza pyramids were spotted and recorded.

Tourism, which is very important to the economy of Egypt, has its own hazards. Visitors to sites and monuments, even if they are careful, accelerate erosion and raise humidity and salinity through the condensation from their breath. Large tour groups tend to crowd into a limited number of monuments, which are overwhelmed by their generally uncontrolled visits; many touch the walls and/or take flash pictures, both very destructive actions. Certain important sites, such as the tomb of

Nefertari in the Valley of the Queens, have had to be closed to tourists. At Giza I have instituted a rotation system so that each pyramid is closed for one year out of three for restoration and conservation.

Excavation poses its own hazards to a site. The simple fact is that once a site has been uncovered, it is automatically exposed to the depredations of polluted air and scouring winds. Archaeologists now routinely backfill sites to protect them from

Hag Ahmed Youssef, the great Egyptian conservator

the elements.

Foreign archaeologists have led the way in terms of new methods of excavation and new technologies; many of them are also participating actively in our attempts to develop and implement effective site management programs. Under their direction, a number of sites have been uncovered or reexplored over the past five decades. Many of these great European and American excavators, in addition to knowing about spectacular artifacts, have unearthed important pieces of art, some of which are featured here.

More and more excavations in Egypt, however, are carried out by well-trained Egyptian teams working directly for the SCA or for Egyptian universities. Over the past 50 years, three generations of Egyptian archaeologists have followed in the footsteps of Ahmed Kamal and Selim Hassan. In the first generation came archaeologists such as Ahmed Fakhry (1905–1973), who did groundbreaking work at Dahshur and in the western oases. Fakhry joined the Antiquities Service in 1932, and in 1938 was appointed chief inspector of Middle Egypt. He published widely, and his handbook of the pyramids of the Old and Middle Kingdoms is still a classic reference work. In addition to his reputation for scholarship, Fakhry was known as an excellent excavator.

The first generation of great Egyptian archaeologists is also well represented by Abdel Moneim Abu Bakr (1907–1976), who was one of the first Egyptian scholars to receive his doctorate in Egyptology—studying in Germany with the great linguist Kurt Sethe—and who went on to teach at Cairo and Alexandria Universities. He never worked for the Antiquities Service, focusing instead on teaching as well as excavating. In 1965 I was privileged to be one of his students. Most of the Egyptian scholars who now teach at Cairo University were also his students.

Other important Egyptian Egyptologists of the mid-20th century were Labib Habichi (1906–1984); Kamal el Mallakh (1918–1987), who discovered the solar boat of Khufu at Giza; the great restorer Hag Ahmed Youssef (1912–1999), who reconstructed Khufu's boat; and Zakaria Ghoneim (1911–1959), who found the unfinished pyramid of Sekhemkhet at Saqqara.

These men trained a second generation of Egyptian archaeologists: Ali Radwan (1941–), who excavated primarily at Abusir and who taught excavation techniques and Egyptian art at Cairo University; Gaballa Ali Gaballa (1939–), my predecessor as secretary-general of the SCA; Said Tawfik (1936–1990), who excavated at Saqqara and led the EAO for a number of years; Ahmed Moussa (1934–1998), who worked both at Saqqara and at Memphis; and Fekri Hassan, who now holds Petrie's chair at University College London. Hassan is one of the top scholars in Predynastic archaeology and currently excavates in the delta.

The difficulties faced by the men of these two generations—who, especially if they were part of the Antiquities Service, were responsible not only for excavating, publishing, and teaching, but also for endless amounts of administration and diplomacy—is illustrated by the death of Zakaria Ghoneim.

President Abdel Nasser visits the Unfinished Pyramid of Sekhemkhet at Saqqara with its excavator, Zakaria Ghoneim, 1954.

This great man drowned himself in the Nile after being held responsible for the disappearance of an artifact from the storerooms at Saqqara; less than a week later, the artifact was found.

There was a period of several decades in which the best Egyptian scholars became more interested in teaching and publishing than in excavating, and few Egyptian archaeologists were numbered among the international elite. Perhaps the last great Egyptian excavator was Shafiek Faried, followed by Ahmed es-Sawy, under whom I was trained at Kom Abu Billo in the 1970s.

I have continued to excavate, though, and am now being joined by the next generation. Featured in this chapter are some of the great pieces found by our native teams, many of which have been hidden away in storerooms and have received little attention from the public at large.

Reclaiming Our Past

Bronze
Height 37 cm
Unprovenanced

IN 1983 A NEW LAW WAS ISSUED THAT BANNED ANY SELLING OF ANTIQUITIES
on Egyptian soil and allowed the SCA to take away unprovenanced objects found
after the UNESCO convention of 1972 without compensation. All antiquities
dealers were forced to give us catalogs of their antiquities and to close their busi-
nesses. We now have more than 30 dealers who have registered their antiquities
with us. Eleven of these have written to me offering to return their illegal objects,
of which there are thousands. We are now building a new storeroom for these
reclaimed treasures.

One of the most important antiquities dealers in Egypt was Abdu el Rahaman
el Sadik, a dealer from the Sharqqiyyeh province of the eastern delta. After the new
law was passed, he registered his pieces and then gave a number of them to the
EAO. This cat was one of the donated objects.

It is a life-size bronze, dating probably from the 26th dynasty (664 B.C. to 525
B.C.), when such statues were very popular. Many examples of this type of cat statue have been found at Tell Basta (also known as Bubastis and Zagazig) in the delta,
the site of a major temple to the goddess Bastet. She was the daughter of the sun
god and a protective goddess. In addition to the Bastet temple, in which cats such
as the one illustrated here were placed as votive objects, extensive cemeteries containing the burials of cats sacrificed, mummified, and dedicated to Bastet have
been found at the site.

Even before its association with Bastet (which occurred at least by the Third
Intermediate period), the cat was important to ancient Egyptians. Many examples
of pet cats, shown with their owners, are known from tombs. The cat was the natural enemy of the snake, which was the adversary of creation and agent of the chaos
that constantly threatened the Egyptian cosmos. Cats are often seen in vignettes
from the funerary literature of ancient Egypt holding knives and killing snakes.

PAIR STATUE OF MAN AND WIFE
Painted limestone
Man: Height 65 cm; Width 16 cm
Wife: Height 63 cm; Width 8 cm
Giza, Old Kingdom
Excavations of Abu Bakr, 1949–53

1950: Unique Statues of the Old Kingdom

BETWEEN 1939 AND 1953 ABU BAKR CARRIED OUT IMPORTANT EXCAVA-
tions at Giza, concentrating especially in the mastaba field west of the Great
Pyramid. He built a rest house for Cairo University in the shadow of the second
pyramid, which he used for teaching and also as a dig house. A number of unique
Old Kingdom sculptures were found in the course of the excavations; Abu Bakr
used an old tomb as a storeroom in which to keep these safe. Unfortunately, he
died before he could publish more than one volume about his work, and most of
the information he collected has remained unavailable to other scholars.

One of Abu Bakr's students was Tohfa Handoussa, who now teaches at Cairo
University. Aware of the importance of her mentor's discoveries, Handoussa
invited American Egyptologists Ed Brovarski and Leonard Lesko from Brown
University to work with her to complete the publication of these tombs. Brovarski
brought a team to Giza and began reclearance of Abu Bakr's concession in the
Western Cemetery of Khufu. He also reopened the tomb where the artifacts were
stored and brought these masterpieces, forgotten for 25 years, back into the light
of day. We put a number of the sculptures found by Abu Bakr in the Hidden
Treasures exhibit; three of them are illustrated here.

STATUE OF SEATED SCRIBE
Painted limestone
Height 46.5 cm; Width of torso 23.5 cm
Dynasty 5
Giza, Western Cemetery
Excavations of Abu Bakr, circa 1950

THE MOST IMPRESSIVE OF THE STATUES FOUND BY ABU BAKR IS THIS seated scribe, the image of an important official of the Old Kingdom. The scribe was crucial to the proper functioning of ancient Egyptian society. To be literate was to be a member of the elite, privy to the inner workings of both palace and temple, and every Egyptian official was, first and foremost, a scribe. At first, only royal princes could be depicted as scribes; later in the Old Kingdom, other officials high up in the government had themselves depicted in the traditional scribal pose, seated cross-legged on the ground, holding a papyrus unrolled on their laps. More than 50 scribal statues from the Old Kingdom are now known to us, and this numbers among the best.

The balance of forms is perfect: The face, with its inlaid eyes, is elegant and serene; the painted details are applied with skill and care. The scribe, whose name unfortunately was not inscribed on the statue, holds his right hand closed, as if to grasp a reed brush for writing. He looks as if he is dreaming. Some of the text, which was painted in black on the papyrus across his lap, can still be seen. The style of this statue dates it to the middle of the 5th dynasty.

There are two other particularly beautiful scribal statues known: One at the Cairo Museum looks like a novice, holding a papyrus in his hand and waiting as if for the words of the king. A scribe in the Louvre looks like a wise, experienced writer.

SERVANT STATUE
Painted limestone
Height 29 cm; Width 13.5 cm
Dynasty 5
Giza, Western Cemetery
Excavations of Abu Bakr, circa 1950

THE WALLS OF ANCIENT EGYPTIAN TOMB CHAPELS ARE OFTEN COVERED
with brightly colored depictions of men and women doing the mundane tasks that
guaranteed the eternal survival of the deceased—sowing and harvesting grain,
baking bread, and making beer, and doing other jobs that provided magically for
the sustenance of the dead. Servant statues such as the one depicted here first
appear in the 4th dynasty; they served the same function as the wall decorations.
In the 5th dynasty, wood replaces stone for this type of image. The servant shown
here is grinding grain to make flour for bread, one of the main staples of the
Egyptian diet.

PAIR STATUE OF IPSEKH AND HENUS
Painted limestone
Height of man 65 cm; Height of wife 51.5 cm
Dynasty 5
Giza, Western Cemetery
Excavations of Abu Bakr, circa 1950

THIS STATUE DEPICTS A MAN NAMED IPSEKH AND HIS WIFE, HENUS, seated on a simple backless chair. Both held priestly titles: Ipsekh was a priest of Khufu, and Henus, like many women at Giza, was a priestess of Hathor. Thus they both served in the royal mortuary cult, Ipsekh for Khufu himself, and Henus for one or more of the queens who were traditionally identified with Hathor. In contrast to the statues of Rahotep and Nofret (pages 38–39), Henus is much smaller than her husband, an indication of their relative status. Henus wears a short wig and a simple tight dress; Ipsekh also wears a short wig and is clad in a short kilt. In his left hand he holds a folded cloth, symbol of his office, against his chest. By his left leg is their son; their daughter embraces his right leg. Such family groups are typical of Old Kingdom statuary.

BENT PYRAMID OF SNEFERU
Dynasty 4, reign of Sneferu
Dahshur

1952: Saving Sneferu

FAKHRY'S MOST FAMOUS DISCOVERIES WERE MADE AT DAHSHUR, THE site of two of Sneferu's pyramids (circa 2575–2551 B.C.). He had been working at the southern of the two, the Bent Pyramid, since 1951. When the excavation season opened in 1952, he began by tracing the line of the pyramid's causeway east to a large area covered with limestone chips, hoping that the remains of the king's valley temple, assumed to have been carried away as building stone in later times, might be found there. On October 16, 1952, he divided the workmen into two gangs and set them to work to begin clearing the deep sand, expecting to find little, and that only after weeks of work. At 8:20 in the morning, after less than an hour and a half of work, a high wall began to emerge from its overlay of sand. The entire valley temple was there, standing to a good height, and Fakhry was able to trace its plan completely. He also recovered statues, stelae, and many other objects, most impressive among which were beautifully carved wall reliefs, many of them bearing the name of Sneferu.

The photograph on the facing page shows the Bent Pyramid of Sneferu from the vantage point of the floodplain to the east. Structural issues encountered by the ancient architects and engineers during construction left the pyramid with the anomalous shape seen here: The pyramid was begun at a steep slope of about 60 degrees. However, the bedrock on which the foundation had been laid proved unstable, so the engineers added a girdle around the core, with a slope of about 55 degrees. In order to finish the structure safely, the slope was reduced even further, to between 43 and 44 degrees.

1976: Model for a Royal Burial

Dahshur, primarily in the Old Kingdom pyramid complexes of Sneferu, but he has also worked among the Middle Kingdom pyramids. His team found this unique piece in November 1976 in the southwest corner of the valley temple of the 12th dynasty king Amenemhat III, underground, in a rock-cut room tunneled out of the bedrock.

Model houses had been discovered before, as part of the furnishings of some Middle Kingdom tombs, but this is the first three-dimensional royal tomb model ever found. The outer surfaces of the model are polished, but the inner surfaces were left rough, suggesting that this is a scale model designed to aid the royal architects in the planning and excavation of a king's sepulchre. The chambers here resemble most closely those beneath the second pyramid of Amenemhat III, at Hawara near the Faiyum Oasis. It is possible that during construction of the Dahshur pyramid of this king, or after it was completed, the king's chief architect had this model made to serve as a blueprint for the next major construction project.

MODEL OF A ROYAL TOMB
Limestone
Height 2.72 cm; Width 11 cm;
  Length 36 cm
Dynasty 12
Dahshur, Valley Temple of
  Amenemhat III

STELA OF NESWENNEFER (LEFT)
Limestone
Height 20 cm; Width 14.1 cm;
  Thickness 3.6 cm
Thought to be dynasty 25, 747–664 B.C.
Saqqara, Serapeum
Excavations of M. Ibrahim Aly, 1982–85

SERAPEUM STELA OF PA KA (RIGHT)
Limestone
Height 16.1 cm; Width 9.3 cm;
  Thickness 2.4 cm
Dynasty 26 (664–525 B.C.)
Saqqara, Serapeum
Excavations of M. Ibrahim Aly, 1982–85

1982–85: More Treasures from the Serapeum

DESPITE MARIETTE'S EARLY EXCAVATIONS AND VARIOUS EXPLORATIONS carried out over the years, the Serapeum had not yet given up all of its secrets. In work carried out between 1982 and 1985, Mohammed Ibrahim Aly, who was then chief inspector at Saqqara, made some important discoveries. Of great interest is some funerary furniture belonging to Prince Khaemwaset, a son of Ramses II known to have carried out restorations to the monuments of his ancestors. Mariette thought that Khaemwaset was buried in the Serapeum, and these new finds suggest that he may have been right. In addition to this furniture, Aly found a number of votive stelae that had been missed in the earlier explorations. The two stelae shown here, along with several others, were chosen to be part of the Hidden Treasures exhibit.

The beautiful stela shown opposite probably dates from the 25th dynasty (747 B.C. to 664 B.C.). It is carved on both sides. Here we can see the sacred Apis bull, a sun disk set between its horns, on a red base. The name of the dedicator, Neswennefer, has been carved in hieroglyphs in front of the bull; a longer text is painted below in a cursive form of hieroglyphs.

The stela pictured above was dedicated by a man named Paka, who lived during the 26th dynasty (664 B.C to 525 B.C.). The Apis bull is seen here inside his sacred boat, in which he was ritually and symbolically transported. Paka himself is shown in the second register, raising his arms in adoration of the divine animal.

WOMAN WITH SISTRUM

Limestone.
Height 25.5 cm; Width 17.5 cm; Thickness 3.8 cm
Late Dynasty 18 or early Dynasty 19
Saqqara, Serapeum
Excavations of M. Ibrahim Aly, 1986

VOTIVE STELAE WERE NOT THE ONLY ARTIFACTS FOUND BY ALY IN HIS clearance work at the Serapeum. He discovered this limestone relief fragment in the debris of the Lesser Vaults, the corridor system begun by Ramses II for the burial of the Apis bulls. It was once part of a scene carved into the chapel of a tomb and bears the hallmarks of the curvilinear, organic, and sensuous style of the late 18th dynasty. The execution here is excellent, and the artist has succeeded in combining the low relief in which the entire figure is carved with raised relief for certain details, such as the face. Although we have no information about the tomb from which this originally came, the woman was most likely a priestess, as she holds a Hathor-headed *sistrum* (musical rattle) and wears a *menat* (necklace), both used in religious ceremonies.

FRAGMENT OF A COFFIN
Basalt
Height 30 cm; Width 20 cm
Late Dynasty 18, possibly reign of
 Amenhotep III
Saqqara, Serapeum
Excavations of M. Ibrahim Aly, 1986

THIS FRAGMENTARY COFFIN OF BASALT REPRESENTS A CULMINATION OF the anthropoid type (page 66). Most coffins from the 18th dynasty were made of wood, but stone came into common usage during the reign of Amenhotep III. The style of the piece, with slightly pouting mouth, fleshy lips, softly rounded chin, and wide nose, also suggests a date in the reign of this king. The false beard attached to the chin indicates that the deceased was depicted here as Osiris. Such coffins represent a significant expense, as hard stones such as basalt require expert handling and were reserved for the upper classes. Unfortunately, we do not know the name of the man for whom this coffin was made, but the elegance of the carving speaks to the skill and polish of the artist who created it.

STATUE OF RANEFEREF
Painted limestone
Height 34 cm
Dynasty 5, reign of Raneferef
Abusir, Mortuary temple of Raneferef
Excavations of Miroslav Verner, 1984

1984: The Forgotten King

ABUSIR, WHICH LIES 9.7 KILOMETERS (6 MILES) SOUTH OF GIZA, WAS THE burial ground for the kings of the 5th dynasty. In the 1960s the EAO granted a concession to work at this site to a team from Czechoslovakia. Under the direction of Zbynek Zaba, and after his death of Miroslav Verner, the Czech team has made many wonderful discoveries, including a new pyramid complex belonging to a queen named Khentkawes II and the intact tomb of Iwfaa, a director of the palace during the 26th dynasty.

Verner's team has identified an unfinished pyramid at Abusir as the tomb of Raneferef, a short-lived king of the 5th dynasty about whom little is known. Their work has enabled them to clarify the history of this shadowy period. Raneferef came to the throne in about 2419 B.C. He began construction on his pyramid, just a few meters southwest of his father's complex, but only the first step of the core was completed before his sudden death only three years later. In the small temple against the east face of this structure, the Czech team found an extensive collection of papyri from Raneferef's temple archive—a treasure of information for Egyptologists that complements a similar archive found many years earlier. They discovered many fragments of statues and also found six more or less complete diorite, basalt, limestone, quartzite, and wood statues of the king, one of which is illustrated here. The Czechs also excavated the substructure of the pyramid and found the burial chamber, which contained fragments of a red granite sarcophagus, royal burial equipment, and the king's mummy. The mummy was examined, and the age of the young king at his death was found to be 22 or 23.

This small statue is of limestone, and shows the king seated on a throne, wearing a short, curled wig (from which the royal uraeus, perhaps made of gold, has disappeared), a mustache, and a false beard. In his right hand, which is against his chest, he holds a flail, symbol of Egyptian kingship. Echoing the symbolism seen in the 4th dynasty statue of Khafre, carved a century earlier (page 34), the Horus hawk stands on the throne back behind Raneferef's head, ready to lift him to heaven. The well-preserved stone of this statue has retained much of its original paint, giving the modern viewer an excellent sense of its ancient appearance.

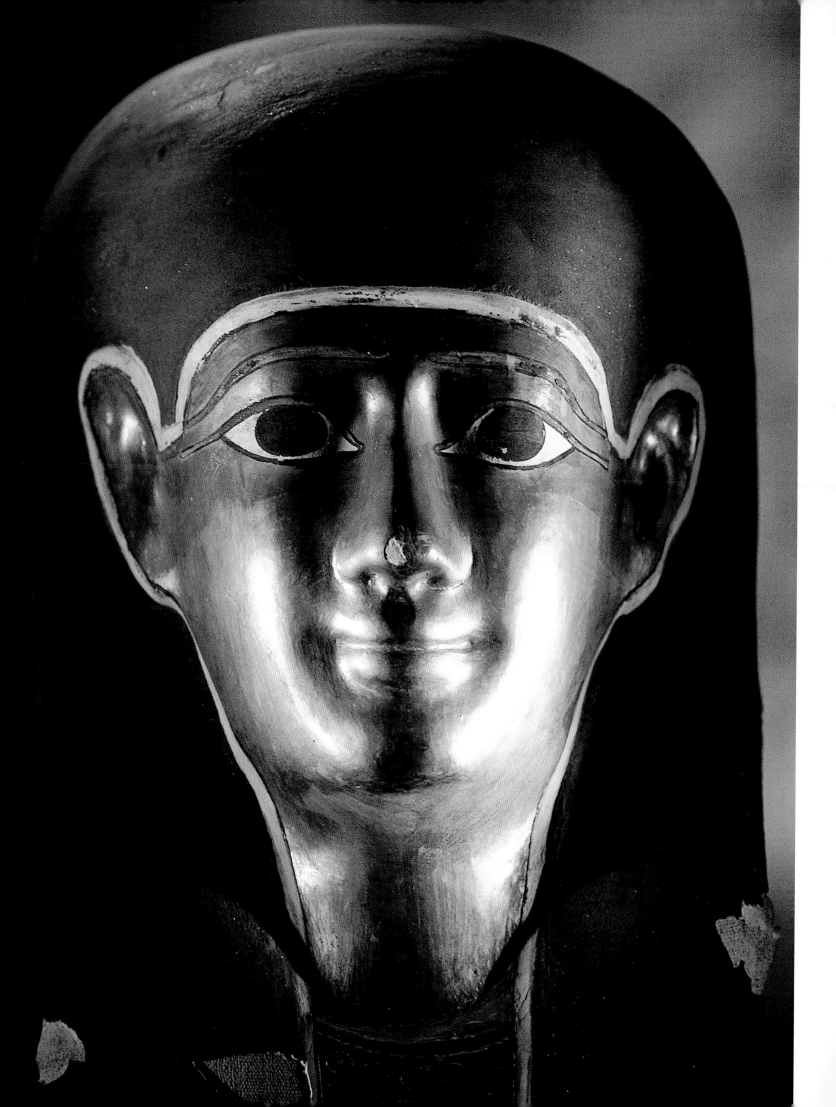

MUMMY MASK
Gilded cartonnage
Height 42.5 cm
Ptolemaic period
Saqqara, Unas Causeway
Excavations of Peter Munro, 1983

1983–1985: Salvage Work at Saqqara

IN THE 1970S A GERMAN EXPEDITION LED BY PETER MUNRO BEGAN excavations north of the causeway of Unas (5th dynasty, circa 2356 B.C. to 2323 B.C.) at Saqqara. Their original work included restoration of the mastabas of two important queens of this period named Neith and Henut that had originally been cleared in 1945. In the course of their explorations, the Germans were able to identify a series of underground galleries as the tomb of Ny-netjer, a king of the 2nd dynasty (circa 2700 B.C.). Mud sealings of this king, along with several others of the same period (in fact, the same three kings whose names were inscribed on the shoulder of Hetepdief, page 46), had been found in this area, and it was hoped that the tombs lay nearby. In autumn 1986 the team began systematically clearing a huge pile of debris near the causeway of Unas, and came across a number of tomb shafts that had penetrated the rock-cut galleries of Ny-netjer's tomb. Hidden in these shafts were a number of fabulous pieces of art dating from various periods of Egyptian history. These are not yet well known to the general public; several were chosen to be part of the Hidden Treasures exhibit.

The wealth of beautiful objects found by Munro stands as a tribute to the richness of the sands at Saqqara. The site is enormous, stretching for many kilometers in the desert west of Cairo, and much of it is still unexcavated. It was used as a cemetery throughout the pharaonic period, and monuments from every period of Egyptian history litter its vast expanse.

Munro found this mummy mask in 1983 in a shaft to the north of a large mastaba. It was inside a rock-cut burial chamber, within a wooden coffin. Thieves had damaged the mummy, and the burial was in terrible condition. But this beautiful mask had escaped the attention of the robbers and survived the millennia intact. It dates to the Ptolemaic period, the era that spans the last three centuries before the birth of Christ, when the heirs of Alexander the Great ruled Egypt. Much Ptolemaic art shows a blend of the Egyptian and Greek traditions. Here the form of the mask is purely Egyptian, illustrating the staying power of the art and iconography of the ancient civilization.

THIS WELL-PRESERVED LIMESTONE STATUE, WITH ONLY THE EARS AND
the snout broken away, depicts the jackal-god Anubis crouching upon a base
shaped like a sarcophagus. It was found within a niche of mud brick, as if stored
for safekeeping. The image brings to mind a similar Anubis figure that was found
in the tomb of Tutankhamun, guarding the entrance to an inner chamber. Anubis
was the god of embalming: A priest wearing a jackal mask and tending to the
mummy is often seen in tomb art. On the base of this statue are carved two lines
of hieroglyphs asking that offerings be given in honor of two royal scribes of the
Treasury named Nefermes and Neferrenpet. Munro has suggested that the statue
might originally have stood in the courtyard of a tomb belonging to a father and
son, two brothers, or two colleagues. One day, perhaps, this tomb will come to
light. The statue has been dated stylistically to the 19th dynasty.

STATUE OF ANUBIS
Limestone
Height 54 cm; Width 25 cm; Length 67 cm
Dynasty 19
Saqqara, Unas Causeway
Excavations of Peter Munro, 1985

**STATUE OF AMENEMIPET
AND HIS WIFE**
Limestone
Height 84 cm; Width 45 cm
Dynasty 19
Saqqara, Unas Causeway
Excavations of Peter Munro, 1985

ONE OF THE MOST BEAUTIFUL OF THE ARTIFACTS FOUND BY MUNRO IS this double statue representing a priest named Amenemipet and his wife. Amenemipet, whose principal title was chief priest of Mut, stands to the right, wearing a curled wig, full and billowing linen garments with pleated sleeves ending in a flare at the elbow, and a pair of sandals. His wife wears a heavy wig that frames her face, topped by a floral diadem. She holds a sistrum in her left hand and embraces her husband with her right. The back of the slab against which the couple leans is fully carved, depicting Amenemipet worshiping Isis and Osiris, and could be considered a work of art in its own right. The clothing worn by the couple is typically Ramesside (i.e., from the 19th or 20th dynasty), a date supported by the general style of the piece.

FALSE DOOR OF KATEPI
Limestone
Height 69 cm; Width 46 cm
Dynasty 6
Saqqara, Unas Causeway
Excavations of Peter Munro, 1985

THIS BEAUTIFUL FALSE DOOR WAS FOUND IN 1985 IN A SHAFT SOUTH OF the mastabas of Queens Neith and Henut. This was one of 34 tomb shafts dug for priests connected with the cult of King Unas in the Old and Middle Kingdoms. The shaft in which this door was found dates to the 11th dynasty, although the door itself is of 6th dynasty date. Katepi was a midlevel official in the central government and bore the titles Sole Companion, Noble of the King, and Scribe of the Office. His principal title was Land Official of Unas-nefersut (the pyramid of Unas, last king of the 5th dynasty), accounting for his burial in the necropolis around the pyramid of this king. The support staff for the cults of the Old Kingdom kings had become quite extensive by this point. In the 4th dynasty, the priestly hierarchy was quite simple, and the staff was relatively small. By the 5th dynasty, and continuing on into the 6th, the number of pyramid cult-related titles proliferates, until a large number of officials have duties toward and receive benefits from the mortuary cults of the kings that had come before them.

This false door would once have been set up within the tomb of Katepi, in a niche above the shaft in which he was buried. From the burial chamber, his spirit would magically have found its way up the shaft and emerged from the central panel of the door to receive offerings, as is depicted on the slab stela above the central panel of the door. Found in the same area as this masterly piece, most likely a product of the royal workshop, were three wooden statues, also from the late Old Kingdom, which represent one person at three phases of life, and the remains of some copper vessels.

1987: The Lost Vizier

ALAN ZIVIE CAME TO EGYPT IN 1969. AFTER FOUR YEARS AS A MEMBER OF the French Institute, he took out a concession to work at Saqqara, in an area known as the Doors of the Cats because of the hundreds of cats buried here during the Late period. He has spent the past three decades working in this rich site, and has uncovered, cleared, and done restoration in more than 25 tombs. The cliff face into which these tombs are carved is extremely friable, and working in this area is quite dangerous and difficult. I spent several months as a young inspector living in the EAO rest house that sits atop this cliff, never dreaming that a wealth of ancient treasures lay below me. Netjerwymes, royal messenger under Ramses II and quite possibly the man who carried the peace treaty between the Egyptians and the Hittites, was buried here, as was Maia, Tutankhamun's wet nurse, along with many others.

The objects shown here come from the tomb of Aperel, who was vizier under Amenhotep III and Amenhotep IV (Akhenaton). The name of this man, which seems to be Semitic rather than Egyptian, had been cut into the face of the cliffs, and his chapel had been identified but left unexplored. It took Zivie seven years to empty the tomb, the largest in the area, of the cats that had been buried there. Excavating this tomb required extra funding to carry out safely. Fortunately, the French were helping to build the Cairo metro at the time; Zivie asked them, along with Cairo University, to study the site, and received the support he needed. Finally, four levels down, he reached the burial chamber, 20 meters (66 feet) underground.

This chamber had been hidden beneath a dummy staircase, but ancient thieves, perhaps even the men who had helped to bury the vizier and his family, had left the room in disarray. There was still much left to find, however, and other scattered artifacts were discovered in the upper levels of the tomb. Illustrated here are some of the most unusual objects from this rich tomb.

The fish of red ivory pictured here functioned as a cosmetic spoon. One face has been carved carefully in the form of the bulti fish *(Tilapia nilotica)*, a common inhabitant of the Nile River. The male of this species carries the fertilized eggs in its mouth until they hatch, at which point they emerge fully developed. This led the ancient Egyptians to associate it with fertility and rebirth. It is also linked with the daily circuit of the sun and the cycle of regeneration.

SPOON IN THE FORM OF A FISH
Ivory
Width 6.1 cm; Length 12 cm
Dynasty 18, reign of Amenhotep III
Saqqara, Tomb of Aperel
Excavations of Alan Zivie, 1987

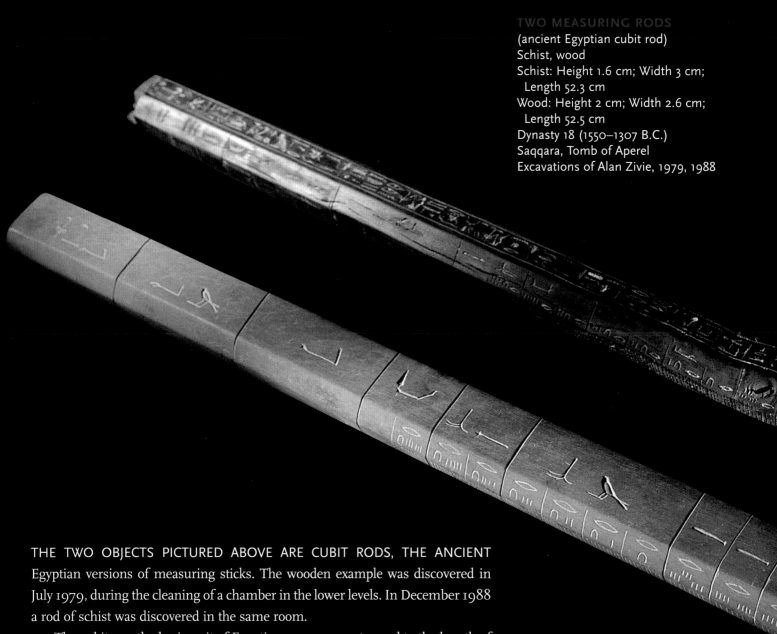

TWO MEASURING RODS
(ancient Egyptian cubit rod)
Schist, wood
Schist: Height 1.6 cm; Width 3 cm;
  Length 52.3 cm
Wood: Height 2 cm; Width 2.6 cm;
  Length 52.5 cm
Dynasty 18 (1550–1307 B.C.)
Saqqara, Tomb of Aperel
Excavations of Alan Zivie, 1979, 1988

THE TWO OBJECTS PICTURED ABOVE ARE CUBIT RODS, THE ANCIENT Egyptian versions of measuring sticks. The wooden example was discovered in July 1979, during the cleaning of a chamber in the lower levels. In December 1988 a rod of schist was discovered in the same room.

The cubit was the basic unit of Egyptian measurement, equal to the length of a forearm. The stone rod is marked with the name and titles of Huy, the eldest son of Aperel. The units on the wooden rod are reversed, running from left to right, suggesting that its owner may have been left-handed. Such rods are often assumed to be votive in nature and unsuitable for daily use, but the inscription on the base of the stone example has been worn away, suggesting that it was handled often.

The unusual piece opposite was found in June 1985, faceup among some debris. The neck was buried, and the workmen thought they had found a funerary mask or coffin. When it was cleaned, it was seen to be a solid wooden head, covered with stucco and painted; it most probably functioned as a wig stand. We know that the Egyptians kept their hair short for coolness and good hygiene and wore wigs for special occasions.

HEAD OF A WOMAN: WIG STAND
Wood
Height 24 cm; Width 16 cm
Dynasty 18, reign of Amenhotep III
Saqqara, Tomb of Aperel
Zivie excavation, circa 1987

STATUE OF THE GOD BES
Limestone
Height 136 cm; Width 60 cm
Late period
Bahariya Oasis, Temple of Bes
SCA excavations, 1988

1988: Bahariya I, The Temple of Bes

THE TEMPLE OF BES AT BAHARIYA WAS DISCOVERED IN 1988, AFTER A villager found a basalt fragment bearing the name of Akhenaton and brought it to Mohamed el-Tayieb, an SCA inspector based in the area. The villager had found it on top of a small mound in the middle of the village of el-Bawiti, the modern capital of Bahariya. Bahariya is one of a string of five oases that lie far out in the western desert. It was important in antiquity as a frontier area, a trading post, and a source of both grape and date wine. There is little or no archaeological evidence here for activity before the New Kingdom, although textual references and other clues suggest that the area was occupied earlier. Most of the remains date from the Late and Greco-Roman periods. The site was neglected by most early explorers, except for a short visit by the circus strongman turned antiquities collector Giovanni Belzoni (1778–1823). Ahmed Fakhry came to Bahariya in the late 1930s and uncovered some important monuments. The site then lay fallow until recently; since 1990, it has become the scene of some very exciting discoveries.

A team from the Bahariya inspectorate, under the direction of Ashry Shaker and the supervision of el-Tayieb, began excavation of the mound on which the inscribed fragment had been found, and uncovered a ruined temple of Bes. This had been built in the Greco-Roman period and destroyed in the early Christian period. This statue was discovered in the main hall of the temple; at the time of its discovery, it had toppled over and lay in front of its base. It clearly served as a cult image, a focal point to which the public could come to present offerings and petitions to the god. The statue depicts Bes in his usual form, as a bandy-legged dwarf with a large, rounded stomach. He is naked except for a belt and a lion skin that falls down his back. Bes was a popular domestic god in ancient Egypt, responsible for keeping evil spirits away and for protecting women during childbirth.

Mohamed el-Tayieb was a good archaeologist and worked with me for several seasons at Bahariya, in the Valley of the Golden Mummies and at Sheikh Soby. We suffered a great loss when he died of a heart attack two years ago.

sied was found at Luxor in 1989. Once again, chance led to the discovery of great treasure. Luxor Temple is one of the gems of ancient Egyptian architecture, much smaller and less imposing than its neighbor, Karnak temple, but more elegant and accessible. By the late 1980s, it was clear that the solar court of Amenhotep III in this temple was in imminent danger: The pillars were moving slowly and the entire structure was in danger of cracking. Under the supervision of Mohammed el Soghair, SCA director of Luxor, scientists came and measured the movements of the pillars, and as part of their work, took soil samples. One morning in January 1989 the workmen taking the samples came across a slab of diorite at a level about 1.8 meters (6 feet) belowground. Recesses on its top surface held two statues. Further excavation began immediately, and the next day this beautiful statue came to light. Two and a half meters (8 feet) under the original block, a number of additional statues were found, including another statue of Amenhotep III; two images of Horemheb with the god Amun; and a figure of Iunyt, goddess of a town called Armant. This discovery was a great event, and President Mubarak flew to Luxor to watch as these beautiful images were brought back into the light of day.

These statues may have been hidden during the Third Intermediate period by loyal priests who wanted to preserve them from harm or alternatively, they might have been buried during the Roman period, when the area was converted into a military camp. Whoever decided to hide them away was successful, as these statues emerged from the earth intact. A further 20 statues, less perfectly preserved, were uncovered over the course of the next month from lower levels of the same pit.

The statue shown here stands 2.5 meters (8 feet) tall and is generally considered one of the most beautiful sculptures ever discovered. The king is seen as an idealized youth, his face childlike. The stone itself seems to glow from within, and the masterly hand of the sculptor has given the king eternal life. Parts of the statue were once gilded.

STATUE OF THE DWARF
PERNIANKHU
Painted basalt
Height 48 cm; Width 14 cm
Dynasty 4
Giza, Western Cemetery
Tomb of Perniankhu
Excavation of Zahi Hawass, 1990

1990: The Dwarf of the Palace

THE NECROPOLIS TO THE WEST OF THE GREAT PYRAMID AT GIZA WAS founded during the reign of Khufu (circa 2589 B.C. to 2566 B.C.) for officials and priests who formed part of his court, and tombs continued to be built here until the end of the Old Kingdom. Most take the form of mastabas, low rectangular structures with sloping sides and flat roofs, laid out in a regular grid pattern of streets and cross streets to form a city of the dead. The burials were in shafts beneath these mastaba superstructures, and inside the larger and more elaborate mastabas are funerary chapels, miniature temples to the cults of the deceased.

The tomb of Perniankhu was discovered in 1990, in clearance operations being carried out at my request by one of my inspectors at Giza, Mahmoud Afifi. I was interested in publishing one of the large tombs in the Western Cemetery, belonging to a high official named Nesutnefer, which had been excavated decades earlier by George Reisner. Debris surrounded the tomb to a height of 5 meters (16 feet), and having assumed that this was material dumped by Reisner, I never dreamed that treasures could lie underneath. But soon after work began, a wall began to emerge from beneath the sand. It belonged to the serdab (enclosed statue chamber) of a tomb. An inscription on the lintel above this room reads, "The King's Acquaintance, the Dwarf of the Palace, Perniankhu," and inside was this beautiful statue.

Perniankhu lived in about 2500 B.C., probably during the reign of Khafre. His upper body here is strong and well proportioned, although the fact that one shoulder is higher than the other suggests that he might have had a slight curvature of the spine. It is his legs that are unusual—they are abnormally short and bowed slightly outward.

Perniankhu is clearly depicted here as a dwarf, a diagnosis that was confirmed by the discovery of his skeleton in a burial shaft below the superstructure of his tomb. Dwarves were not uncommon in ancient Egypt and were often held in high esteem. A traditional function of dwarves in the Old Kingdom was to dance before the king; it is likely that this was at least part of Perniankhu's duties at court. Dwarves also participated in funeral dances and were closely associated with the sun god.

SARCOPHAGUS OF IRETHORWEDJA
Black granite
Height 145 cm; Width 100 cm; Length 241 cm
Dynasty 26
Qiwesna
SCA excavations, 1992

1992: Sarcophagus of Irethorwedja

CURRENT ANTIQUITIES LAW REQUIRES THAT AN SCA TEAM BE PRESENT anytime new construction is undertaken near a known archaeological site. In 1990 work was begun, under SCA supervision, on a building project at Qiwesna in the southern delta, 57 kilometers (34 miles) north of Cairo. This site lies 15 meters (50 feet) above the surrounding fields and is nicknamed Kufur Aramna, "small village of sand." The initial phases of the construction exposed a limestone sarcophagus, some architectural elements, stelae, and human remains. The project was stopped so that proper excavations could be carried out. This work uncovered architectural elements of mud brick belonging to a group of Late period burials. Artifacts recovered included pottery vessels of different sizes, jewelry, shawabtis (funerary statuettes), granite sarcophagi, and alabaster canopic jars.

The black granite sarcophagus shown here was found in 1992 and dates to the 26th dynasty. It is inscribed with 27 lines of hieroglyphic text, including excerpts from the Book of the Dead and the name and titles of the owner. Irethorwedja was connected with the cult of Osiris at nearby Tell Athrib, as was his entire family. The decoration of the sarcophagus is beautifully executed. One scene shows the family standing in front of a sacred tree, and another depicts Anubis inside a mummification tent.

Bringing this massive sarcophagus to Cairo for the Hidden Treasures exhibit was quite an adventure. It weighs about 20 tons and lay on a mound 17 meters (56 feet) high, between architectural features of easily damaged mud brick. My chief architect at Giza, Abd el-Hamied Kotb, brought in Talal and Ahmed el-Kiriti, experts in moving heavy objects using deceptively simple, nondestructive methods, to supervise the move. The el-Kiriti brothers were taught their trade by their father and their father's father, and their techniques date back to ancient times. On the day of the move, after having prepared everything carefully, Abd el-Hamied Kotb's team, under the supervision of the el-Kiriti brothers, tied the sarcophagus with ropes and pulled it onto wooden sledges, using iron bars as levers. Laying down a track of wooden rollers, the workmen dragged the sarcophagus across the site and through a nearby field, chanting together to help keep their movements rhythmic and smooth. The sarcophagus and its lid were carefully padded and loaded into a truck bound for Cairo. It is too big for the exhibit space, so the sarcophagus now sits in the western courtyard of the museum, outside the basement entrance.

STATUE OF KAI
Painted limestone with inlaid crystal eyes
Height 55.9 cm; Width of base 25 cm
Old Kingdom, end of Dynasty 4
Giza, Western Cemetery, tomb of Kai
Excavations of Zahi Hawass, 1992

1992: The Tomb of Kai

I FOUND THIS EXQUISITE STATUE IN 1992 IN THE MASTABA OF KAI, A jewellike tomb located in the Western Cemetery of Khufu, not far from the tomb of Perniankhu (page 151). Kai's chapel comprises a single chamber, beautifully decorated with carefully carved and vibrantly colored scenes.

The focus of the cult, as was traditional in Egyptian tomb chapels, was the western wall, since the dead were believed to reside in the west, in the direction of the setting sun with whom they traveled. This wall was decorated with two "false doors," niches carved to look like the doors of Egyptian houses but with no actual opening. Beneath each false door was a burial shaft. One part of the soul of the deceased was thought magically to leave the burial shaft and emerge through the false door to partake of offerings placed before it. Kai's statue, which functioned as a substitute for his body, was sealed within a serdab located behind one of the two false doors. As we know from inscriptions both in the chapel and on the statue itself, Kai was, among other things, a priest for the cults of Khufu, Khafre, and Djedefre; a senior scribe; and overseer of the *ka*-priests (priests responsible for the funerary cult). A beautifully drawn amulet of turquoise could be seen on his chest, below the faint traces of a broad collar that are still visible, but exposure to the air destroyed it immediately, before it could be preserved. At his feet are two of his many children: A son, who is shown as a child but is old enough to have been awarded the title of Scribe, stands by his right leg in the traditional pose of youth; and a daughter, Nefret, kneels and embraces her father's left leg.

Painted limestone
Seated: Height 75 cm; Width 26 cm
Seated: Height 40.5 cm; Width 12.2 cm
Seated: Height 32 cm; Width unknown
Standing: Height 31 cm; Width 5.8 cm
Old Kingdom, End of Dynasty 4
Giza, Tombs of the Pyramid Builders, Tomb of Inty-shedu
Excavations of Zahi Hawass, 1992

1992: Tombs of the Pyramid Builders

IN SUMMER 1990 A TOURIST WAS HORSEBACK RIDING IN THE DESERT south of the Great Sphinx at Giza when her horse stumbled and threw her. The hole in which the horse's hoof had gotten caught exposed part of a mud-brick wall that, on further investigation by an SCA team under my direction and the supervision of Mansour Boriak, turned out to be part of an ancient tomb. Subsequent excavations have revealed parts of a vast cemetery housing the bodies of the men and women who helped build the pyramids at Giza—the workers from all over the country who toiled to move the great stones; their supervisors; the women who served as support staff; and the artisans and minor officials who organized the great projects and carved the reliefs and statues that decorated the royal temples and the tombs of the elite.

The mastaba tomb of Inty-shedu is located in the upper cemetery, where the higher-ranking men—artisans and minor officials—were buried with their families. These four statues were found inside a serdab sealed with limestone and mud-brick plaster, with only an eyeslit left open. Hieroglyphic labels on these four statues give Inty-shedu's primary title as "Overseer of the Boats of Neith." The largest statue includes the honorific title "King's Acquaintance": It is likely that Inty-shedu was promoted to this rank later in life and had this last and most impressive statue made soon before his death.

American archaeologist Mark Lehner has been working at Giza for several decades and shared my hope of finding traces of the men and women who built the pyramids. In 1991 he began excavating in an area below the cemetery of the pyramid builders, near a large wall called the Wall of the Crow. In the first trenches opened, Mark and his team found a series of Old Kingdom bakeries. In subsequent seasons, with the judicious use of a front-end loader, he and his team have uncovered enormous swaths of an important Old Kingdom settlement—the royal installation and houses of the men and women who helped build the pyramids, the same people who are buried in the tombs above. Between the explorations of the cemetery above and the installation and town below, we are building up a more complete picture of life and death in the Old Kingdom.

1992: The Earliest Writing

THESE BONE LABELS WERE FOUND BY AN EXPEDITION LED BY

Günter Dreyer to Abydos, site of the burials of the earliest Egyptian kings. Dreyer has been excavating at Abydos since 1977. He has concentrated his efforts in the area of the Umm el-Qa'ab, where the kings of the 1st and 2nd dynasties and their predecessors were buried.

The earliest elite tombs at Abydos are in Cemetery U, the northernmost cemetery at the Umm el-Qa'ab, where the Germans have mapped and excavated about 400 Predynastic grave pits and identified several hundred more small empty offering pits from the New Kingdom and later. The earliest tombs are all about the same size, but later there appears a great deal more differentiation in size and elaboration: The bigger tombs are probably for chieftains and what archaeologists call proto-kings.

The largest tomb in Cemetery U, dated through radiocarbon to about 150 years before the beginning of the 1st dynasty, was found in 1988. It has 12 chambers and measures about 8 meters by 6 meters (27 feet by 21 feet). It had been robbed, but the Germans found many important artifacts that had been left behind or missed by earlier excavators. The most impressive was a scepter of ivory in the shape of a crook—one of the most important symbols of ancient Egyptian royalty throughout pharaonic history. This artifact, coupled with the size and elaborate architecture of the tomb, suggests that the person buried here might have been a king. In addition to a great deal of Egyptian pottery, there were more than 200 wine jars imported from abroad, probably from Palestine. There were also 150 small labels of ivory and bone that bore short inscriptions containing from one to four hieroglyphic signs. This is the earliest writing known from Egypt and is contemporary with the earliest writing known from Mesopotamia.

The labels shown here come from the tomb of a king of the 1st dynasty named Qa'a. Labels such as these are some of the most important historical artifacts from the Early Dynastic period. They are usually of wood or, in this case, of ivory or bone, and were attached to objects such as jars or boxes to date them and record their contents. The hieroglyphic signs on labels such as the ones depicted here are somewhat difficult to interpret, as they represent a very early phase of writing. However, enough can be gleaned to provide important information about political, religious, and economic aspects of this period. All four of these labels seem to have been on jars containing fine oils.

WRITTEN LABELS
Bone and ivory
Heights range from 3 cm to 3.4 cm
Widths range from 3.6 cm to 4 cm
Dynasty 1, reign of King Qa'a
Abydos, Umm el-Qab
Excavations of Günter Dreyer, 1992

hills since the early days of exploration in Egypt. All of these are deteriorating at an alarming rate; many of them have never been properly published and may soon be gone forever if nothing is done. A number of teams have been working in the area, reexploring and properly recording these tombs.

The University of Cambridge Theban Mission has been working here since 1984. In 1992 the team, under the direction of British Egyptologist Nigel Strudwick, began work in tomb 99. This is the tomb of an 18th dynasty official named Senneferi, which had never been studied or documented. Five shafts were found in the rear chamber of the tomb, all of which turned out to have been cut in the Third Intermediate period. First to be explored was the central shaft, directly below the offering niche.

In this central shaft, Strudwick's team discovered the well-preserved but headless body of the statue shown here. It is of sandstone and depicts a "deputy overseer of seal-bearers" named Amenhotep. Four days later, the site supervisor, Rachel Walker, found a sandstone head in another of the shafts; this fit perfectly onto the body. The season ended soon after these dramatic events, and the statue was packed and taken to the SCA magazine.

The next season began in December 1994, and work began in the burial chamber at the bottom of one of the shafts. On December 17 two black-painted fragments of sandstone were found, evidently from the wig of a statue. Strudwick was permitted access to the SCA magazine where the statue of Amenhotep was stored and found that the new fragments were indeed part of this figure, which is now 90 percent complete.

This statue must once have stood in the tomb and later been broken and thrown into these two shafts. It is a beautiful piece, displaying great skill on the part of the sculptor. Amenhotep wears a long kilt and a shawl over one shoulder, and he holds a lotus flower, symbol of resurrection, to his breast.

Amenhotep had a tomb of his own nearby, whose location is now lost. In his tomb, his wife is identified as Renena, daughter of the overseer of seal-bearers, Senneferi. Thus Amenhotep chose to commemorate himself with this statue in the tomb of his father-in-law.

1994: The Jewels of Weret

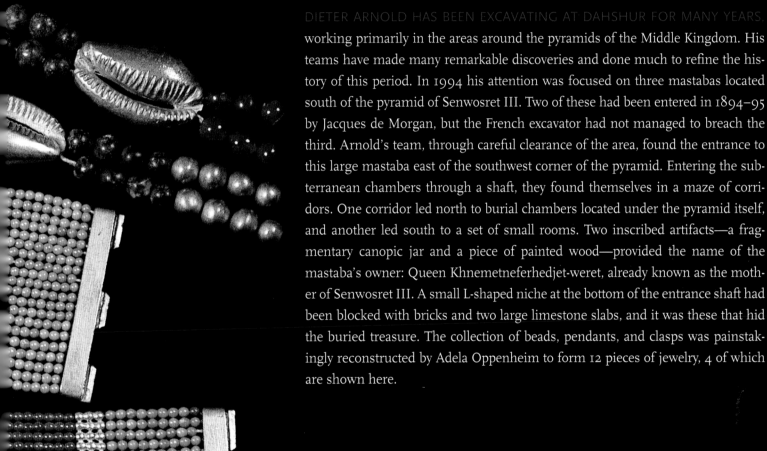

DIETER ARNOLD HAS BEEN EXCAVATING AT DAHSHUR FOR MANY YEARS, working primarily in the areas around the pyramids of the Middle Kingdom. His teams have made many remarkable discoveries and done much to refine the history of this period. In 1994 his attention was focused on three mastabas located south of the pyramid of Senwosret III. Two of these had been entered in 1894–95 by Jacques de Morgan, but the French excavator had not managed to breach the third. Arnold's team, through careful clearance of the area, found the entrance to this large mastaba east of the southwest corner of the pyramid. Entering the subterranean chambers through a shaft, they found themselves in a maze of corridors. One corridor led north to burial chambers located under the pyramid itself, and another led south to a set of small rooms. Two inscribed artifacts—a fragmentary canopic jar and a piece of painted wood—provided the name of the mastaba's owner: Queen Khnemetneferhedjet-weret, already known as the mother of Senwosret III. A small L-shaped niche at the bottom of the entrance shaft had been blocked with bricks and two large limestone slabs, and it was these that hid the buried treasure. The collection of beads, pendants, and clasps was painstakingly reconstructed by Adela Oppenheim to form 12 pieces of jewelry, 4 of which are shown here.

**STATUE OF NEB-RE AS STANDARD-BEARER
OF THE GODDESS SEKHMET**
Sandstone
Height 123.5 cm
Dynasty 19, reign of Ramses II
Zawiet um el Rakhem
Joint SCA/Liverpool excavations, 1994

1994: Defending the Western Borders

THE SITE OF ZAWIET UM EL RAKHEM LIES ALONG THE MEDITERRANEAN coast at the extreme western edge of the Egyptian delta, 28 kilometers (17 miles) west of Mersa Matruh. It was first explored in 1925 by Anthony Decoson, and in 1946 by Alan Rowe, a close associate of George Reisner's. Labib Habichi worked here in 1955 as part of his explorations of the military fortresses that protected the western border of Egypt. The fortress at Zawiet um el Rakhem was founded during the reign of Ramses II, who was concerned with securing this crucial border, vulnerable to attack by the Libyan tribes to the west. During the reigns of his successors, these tribes, along with various displaced groups known collectively as the Peoples of the Sea, succeeded in mounting a serious threat to the integrity of the borders of Egypt. Although they were repulsed at this point, Libyans had infiltrated the delta in sufficient numbers by the Third Intermediate period to take over primary rule of Egypt as the 21st and 22nd dynasties.

In 1994 a team from Liverpool University, in conjunction with the SCA, carried out excavations within the 15,000-meter-square fortress that commands the site. The team discovered architectural components belonging to a number of buildings contained within the fortress. One of these was a temple, built against the western wall of the fort. Near this temple were three rooms, and in one of these rooms the team found a cachette—a purposefully hidden group of objects—containing this beautiful statue, along with four other pieces.

The statue represents Nebre, the commander of the fortress under Ramses II. He wears his military uniform and holds in one hand his staff of office, topped by the head of Sekhmet, lioness-headed goddess of war and consort of Ptah, god of Memphis and patron of craftsmen.

NAOS OF PTAH AND SEKHMET
Sandstone
Height 90 cm
Dynasty 19, reign of Ramses II
Zawiet um el Rakhem
Joint SCA/Liverpool excavations, 2000

2000: Naos of Ptah and Sekhmet

THIS NAOS, OR FREESTANDING SHRINE, IS A BEAUTIFUL EXAMPLE OF ITS type. Naoi could be made of wood or stone, and contained cult images of deities. They could be kept inside a temple sanctuary or set up outside the temple to provide a divine focus for those not admitted to the inner sanctum. This naos contains images of Ptah and his consort Sekhmet carved in very high relief, almost detached from the back wall. Although the shrine itself is cut roughly, the gods are elegantly crafted, although now much weathered. Ptah, god of craftsmen, was the patron god of Memphis and an important deity in the Egyptian pantheon. According to one version of the creation myth, Ptah was the original creator god, and stood on the primeval mound that first emerged from the waters of chaos to bring the world into being. Sekhmet was a lioness-goddess, patroness of war.

SARCOPHAGUS OF SENQED

Black granite
Width 52 cm; Length 175 cm
Late Dynasty 18 to early Dynasty 19
Saqqara
Excavations of Magdi el-Ghandour, 1994

1994: Dressed for Eternal Life

THIS BEAUTIFUL SARCOPHAGUS WAS FOUND BY ACCIDENT IN 1994 AT Saqqara, at the bottom of an 8-meter-deep (27-foot) shaft south of the tomb of Horemheb (last king of the 18th dynasty), who built this large and elegant tomb before he ascended to the throne, and then abandoned it in favor of burial in the Valley of the Kings. The man who first saw this piece was a reis working under the supervision of Magdi el-Ghandour, who was at the time the chief inspector of Saqqara. Everyone thought that they had found the head of a large statue, but their curiosity and excitement had to be put on hold for five days, until the celebration of a Coptic feast called the Biram was over and the team could return to work. When the piece was excavated, it was seen to be the lid of this exquisite coffin of basalt, which belonged to a man named Senqed. The base was also found in fragments, which have been reconstructed around a Lucite base by Ahmed Orabi (OVERLEAF).

Senqed is known to have built a tomb at a site now called Awlad Azzaz, making the appearance of his sarcophagus at Saqqara rather unusual. His name has been scratched out wherever it appears, making it most likely that someone, perhaps the owner of the tomb shaft in which it was found, brought it here to use for his own burial. The unusual coffin type seen here, where the deceased is shown in the dress of the living rather than the mummy wrappings of death, dates the piece to the late 18th or early 19th dynasty. The inner coffins of Sennedjem and his wife (pages 44–45) were also in this form. The beauty of the carving suggests strongly that the sarcophagus came from the royal workshop at Memphis.

N 1995 A WATER PIPE WAS BEING INSTALLED IN THE VILLAGE OF GEZIRET Mutaway in the governate of ash-Sarqiyyah. While trenches in which to lay the pipe were being dug, three limestone sarcophagi turned up. Work stopped immediately, and experts from the SCA were called in. Two of the sarcophagi had been broken during the trenching, but the other was still in good shape. Scientific excavations at Geziret Mutaway began in March 1995, uncovering tombs and sarcophagi, dating mostly to the Third Intermediate and Late periods.

These four canopic jars had been placed carefully around one of the first sarcophagi to appear. They held the viscera of a man named Pakeredemamon. Although early canopic jars bore no particular distinguishing features, by the Middle Kingdom they were stoppered with human heads, representations of the deceased whose organs they protected. By the late 18th dynasty a new style of stoppers had been introduced, representing divine beings known as the four sons of Horus. The tops of these jars depict the human head of Imsety, the baboon head of Hapy, the jackal head of Duamutef, and the falcon head of Qebehsenuef. Each of them was destined to protect the contents of one specific jar: Imsety guarded the liver, Hapy the lungs, Duamutef the stomach, and Qebehsenuef the intestines.

CANOPIC JARS OF PAKEREDEMAMON
Hapy: Height 43 cm
Imsety: Height 50 cm
Qebehsenuef: Height 53 cm
Duamutef: Height 45 cm
Ash-Sarqiyyah, Geziret Mutaway
SCA salvage excavation, 1995

NURSE STATUE
Limestone
Height 81.7 cm
Bubastis
Accidental find, A. Hassanein, 1998

1996: Nurse of the Royal Children

THIS UNUSUAL STATUE, DEPICTING A WOMAN WITH FOUR ROYAL children, was found near Bubastis. It was discovered when a local man began digging foundations for a new house. The chief inspector of Bubastis, Louis Labieb Boles, sent in a team that carefully brought the statue out of the muddy ground in which it was lying. After being kept for several days in the nearby town of Zagazig for cleaning, the statue was brought to the Cairo Museum. The chief restorer and his staff spent three weeks cleaning and drying the statue, which was waterlogged from its sojourn in the wet ground of the delta.

The central figure of the statue shows a mature woman seated on a chair. With her are four royal children. Three of the children stand against her chest, and the fourth, a princess, sits across her lap. The statue was once painted, and traces of color still remain. Most striking are the metal and stone inlays that have survived the ravages of time. The pedestal had once been inscribed with a hieroglyphic text, but this has now been erased. The style of the carving and the details of clothing and hairstyle date this piece to the mid 18th dynasty, to the reign of Tuthmosis III or Amenhotep II. Egyptian scholar Mohammed Saleh compares it to a similar statue of Queen Huy, mother of the principal wife of Tuthmosis III, who is shown with her five grandchildren.

SCHIST COSMETIC PALETTE
Height 23 cm; Width 12.5 cm;
 Depth 0.8 cm
Predynastic period, Naqada III
Minshat Ezzat, El-Sinbellaween
SCA excavations under Salem Gabra
El Bagdady, 1998

THE VILLAGE OF MINSHAT EZZAT IS LOCATED ABOUT 25 KILOMETERS (15 miles) to the south of Mendes, in the eastern delta. An important tell dominated the area through the first half of the 20th century; this has now been almost completely destroyed by the people from the surrounding villages, who have carried away much of the sand and dirt to build dams. Kamal el-Tawiel, a famous Egyptian composer, owns a parcel of land near the village. When he began to find ancient artifacts on his estate, he immediately notified the authorities. Antiquities law states that if someone buys a piece of property knowing that it may contain antiquities and antiquities are in fact discovered, he or she may be responsible for financing excavations on the land. It was immediately clear that el-Tawiel had stumbled on an important site, so the SCA came in to carry out excavations; el-Tawiel paid for this work himself.

Work began in September 1998, under archaeologist Salem Gabra El Bagdady of the SCA. Almost immediately, the team unearthed a settlement and a large cemetery of mud-brick tombs dating to the Predynastic and Early Dynastic periods. Perhaps for religious or political reasons, the site was destroyed sometime in the 1st dynasty, as indicated by a layer of ashes. A number of the Predynastic and Early Dynastic tombs at the site were extremely rich and contained beautiful objects, some of which are illustrated here.

This beautiful shield-shaped slate palette, an excellent example of its type, dates to the end of the Predynastic period. It is small enough to be held with one hand, and would probably have been set on the dressing table of a wealthy Egyptian. Although it shows no signs of use, it was designed for grinding pigment, which would have been placed in the round area in the center formed by the necks of two fantastic creatures. The style and subject matter of the carving show connections with the contemporary art of Mesopotamia. The left top edge of the palette is formed by the back of some sort of grazing animal, who stands on its hind legs to reach the leaves of the palm tree in front of it (a very Mesopotamian motif). The types of animals on this palette—dogs, gazelles, hares, and various fantastic animals—appear in tomb decoration throughout the pharaonic period in scenes depicting desert hunts and have symbolic overtones connected with the sun (the desert is the place where the sun both rises and sets), fertility, and rebirth. The eye paint ground on palettes such as this one had both practical and religious purposes.

COSMETIC SPOON
Schist
Length 16.5 cm
Naqada III period (circa 3100 B.C.)
Minshat Ezzat, al-Simbillaween
SCA excavations, 1998

THE LARGE, PERFECTLY CRAFTED SPOON SHOWN HERE IS AN EXCELLENT example of the stonework of the late Predynastic period. Using simple tools, craftsmen were able to create finely polished masterpieces such as this one.

The elegant scimitar-shaped blade shown opposite was found in one of the 1st dynasty tombs. The flint has been carefully worked, and the name of Den, fourth king of the 1st dynasty, is inscribed on the blade. The royal name has been placed inside a rectangular box bordered on the bottom by a series of niches representing the facade of a mud-brick palace of the sort in which the king would probably have lived during his lifetime. Royal funerary enclosures at Abydos and magnificent mastabas at Saqqara, all dating from the Early Dynastic period, also display this sort of elaborate niching, a heritage from Mesopotamian architecture. Above the rectangle, which is known by its ancient Egyptian name of *serekh*, perches Horus, who is both the king's protector and his divine incarnation. The entire image can be read as "Den is in his palace, protected by Horus." The knife itself might have been used to perform ritual sacrifices of sacred animals; similar knives were used throughout the pharaonic period for this purpose.

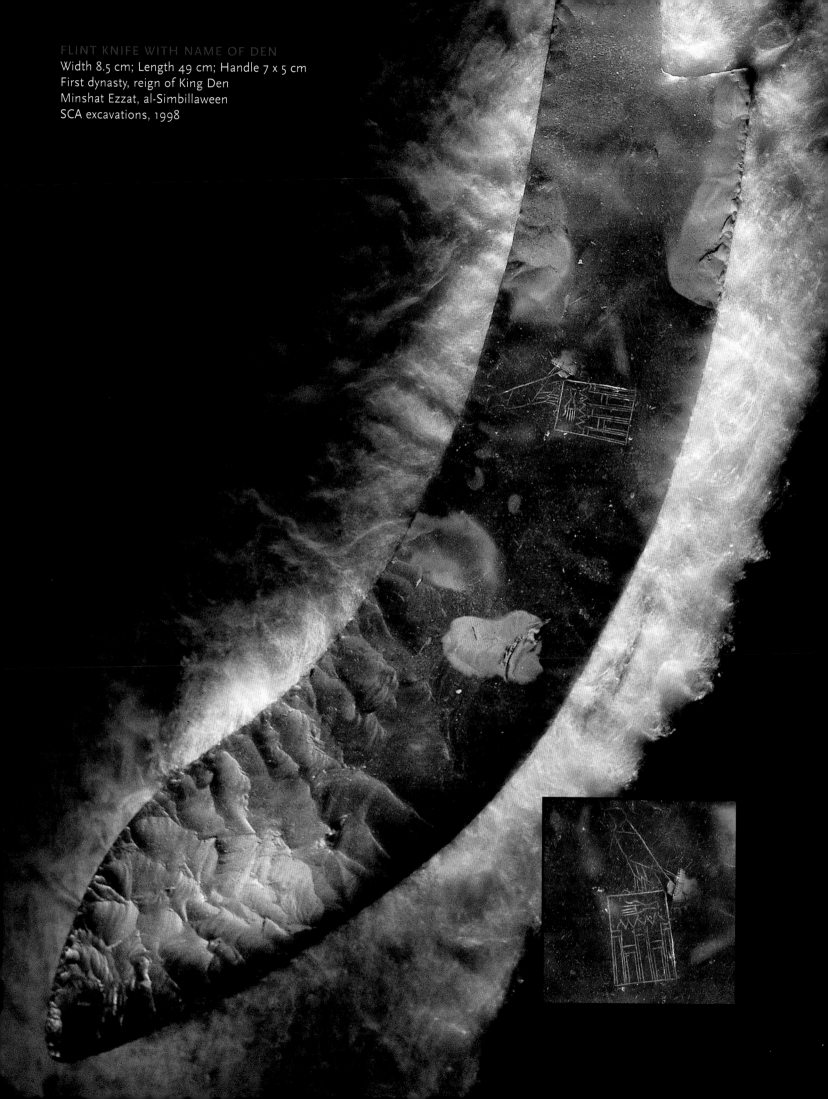

FLINT KNIFE WITH NAME OF DEN
Width 8.5 cm; Length 49 cm; Handle 7 x 5 cm
First dynasty, reign of King Den
Minshat Ezzat, al-Simbillaween
SCA excavations, 1998

1999: Bahariya II
Valley of the Golden Mummies

IN 1996 A DONKEY BELONGING TO A GUARD AT THE TEMPLE OF Alexander in the Bahariya Oasis led his owner to a hole in the desert sand. When the guard peered in, he was blinded by the gleam of gold. When I was informed of this find, I could not believe it, and thought that my assistant, Mansour Boriak, was playing a trick on me. But I was soon convinced that it was true and traveled to Bahariya to see for myself. It took several years of careful preparations before I could bring a carefully selected team to the oasis and begin excavating what has become known as the Valley of the Golden Mummies, a vast necropolis that probably contains more than 10,000 burials.

Over the course of three seasons we found 17 large family tombs, a total of 235 gilded mummies, and a number of priceless artifacts, all dating to the Greco-Roman period. The information that we have already gleaned from this site is extraordinary, and there is much more to come. We have stopped excavation for now to concentrate on more pressing projects, but a vast hoard of treasure still lies beneath the sands.

These two mummies, who were found next to each other in one of these tombs, were very likely brother and sister. The mummy of an adult male, most likely their father, had been laid to rest nearby. The boy was five years old when he died; his sister was four. Both mummies are wrapped in linen, in a geometric pattern characteristic of the Roman period, their heads covered by the gilded and painted masks typical of the site. These two mummies were among the group I chose to move to the Bahariya Museum, so that tourists could see some of the mummies without visiting the tombs and damaging the ancient remains. The children haunted my dreams for several months, until I moved the male mummy whom I believe to be their father to the museum to join them.

AMULET OF QEBEHSENUEF
Gold
Height 9 cm
Dynasty 26 (664–525 B.C.)
Bahariya Oasis, Sheikh Soby, tomb of
  Djed-Khonsu-iufankh
Excavations of Zahi Hawass, 2000

2000: Bahariya III
The Lost Tombs of Sheikh Soby

IN SEPTEMBER 1999 MY TEAM AND I WERE FINISHING UP OUR FIRST season at the Valley of the Golden Mummies near the Bahariya Oasis when two local young men came to me and told me that some villagers were planning to dig for antiquities near the cenotaph of a religious leader named Sheikh Soby that lay in the center of the village of el-Bawiti. Although I did not trust them completely, I asked the chief local inspector to keep watch, and when I was able, I accompanied him. We watched for a month and saw nothing, then one day entered one of the houses and found a hole in the courtyard that led to an ancient tomb! This tomb, and several others, had been discovered decades earlier by the great Egyptian archaeologist Ahmed Fakhry, but then had been lost from sight. A Late period temple at Ain el-Muftelleh (in the oasis) shows the most important members of the governing family of the oasis during the 26th dynasty (664 B.C. to 525 B.C.) on a scale equal to that of the king. From the inscriptions on the walls, a family tree containing at least 13 members can be reconstructed. The tombs found by Fakhry represented some of these family members, but the most important men had not yet been found. Exploration of the tombs found by Fakhry led us to a new burial, this one belonging to the most powerful governor of this period, Djed-Khonsu-iufankh.

This solid-gold amulet was among the objects recovered from the burial chamber of Djed-Khonsu-iufankh himself. Designed to magically protect the body, it would originally have been placed inside the wrappings of the mummy. Here the falcon-headed god Qebehsenuef is depicted as a mummy, standing and holding the feather of Ma'at (representing the proper order of the Egyptian universe) and some strips of linen of the sort that would have been used for wrappings. Qebehsenuef was one of the four sons of Horus, protective deities responsible for guarding the viscera of the deceased. The entire figure can perhaps be read as a desire that the mummy of Djed-Khonsu-iufankh be prepared correctly and effectively. Also visible in the photograph is a small scarab amulet.

The chambers of this tomb led us to another tomb, the tomb of Djed-Khonsu-iufankh's father, and then to the tomb of his wife. We have continued to explore this area and discover more tombs; three potentially intact burials still wait to be opened in our next season.

MASK
Pottery
Height 25 cm; Width 19.8 cm
Late Predynastic or Early Dynastic
  period (circa 3200–3000 B.C.)
Hierakonpolis
Excavations of Renee Friedman and
  Barbara Adams, 1999–2000

1999-2000: Hierakonpolis II
New Explorations

SINCE THE DAYS OF QUIBELL AND GREEN THE SITE OF HIERAKONPOLIS (ancient Nekhen) has been the focus of much archaeological activity. The list of archaeologists who have worked here includes Michael Hoffman, an expert on Predynastic Egypt. Hoffman had dedicated his life to his work at Nekhen but died in 1990, before he could finish what he had planned to do. Since this time, three expeditions have gone to Hierakonpolis under the leadership of Barbara Adams and Renee Friedman.

The early days of Egyptology were not particularly friendly to women, and the field has been dominated by men for most of its history. Over the course of the past 50 years, though, more and more women have been following in the footsteps of early female Egyptologists such as Margaret Murray (1863–1963) and Gertrude Caton-Thompson (1888–1985); these scholars are making important contributions to the field. However, although many female archaeologists have been important members of fieldwork teams (William Flinders Petrie's wife, Hilda, for example was indispensable to her husband), they have been and continue to be more often assistants to male expedition leaders. This is changing slowly, especially among the foreign missions; the number of female archaeologists within the SCA is still extremely small, although there are a number of female Egyptian Egyptologists who hold important posts in Egyptian universities or museums.

This ancient mask was one of a group of similar pieces found by Adams and Friedman in a Predynastic cemetery at Hierakonpolis. It is probably a primitive funerary mask and shows that the Egyptians were already concerned at this early date with providing alternative forms of identification in case the real body of the deceased was destroyed.

FLINT ANIMALS

Hippopotamus: Height 4.8 cm;
  Width 11.4 cm;
Ibex: Height 20 cm; Width 6.9 cm
Late Predynastic or Archaic period
Hierakonpolis
Hippo: Excavations of Michael
  Hoffman, 1979
Ibex: Excavations of Adams and
  Friedman 1999–2000

MICHAEL HOFFMAN FOUND THIS FLINT HIPPO IN 1979 WHILE MAKING A map of the site of Hierakonpolis. Barbara Adams and Renee Friedman discovered the ibex in the same area in 1999-2000. The hippopotamus and the ibex were both symbols of the chaotic regions that surrounded Egypt and continually threatened the existence of Ma'at—the proper order of things. The hippopotamus was a representation of disorder and an incarnation of the god Seth, who was the enemy of Horus; a number of temple and tomb scenes show the king or the tomb owner as Horus harpooning a hippopotamus and thus symbolically maintaining order over chaos. The ibex was a denizen of the desert, a chaotic realm.

The work that Friedman (Barbara Adams died in 2002) is doing at Hierakonpolis is fascinating. In 1997, during salvage excavations along the southeastern edge of the site, her team found 60 complete Predynastic burials. These had been robbed immediately after interment, clearly by thieves who knew exactly what they were seeking. The bodies were wrapped in matting and linen; the most common artifacts found with them were simple pots. Most of the burials were intact except for damage to the head and neck area, where whatever the robbers were looking for must have been located. In some cases, the only evidence for the activities of the thieves is a small slit in the matting above the neck. Although these burials are poor in terms of funerary goods, they provide a wealth of information in the form of well-preserved organic remains—the bodies themselves, which were naturally mummified by the sand in which they were laid, and the baskets, contents of pots, mats, and cloth with which they were found.

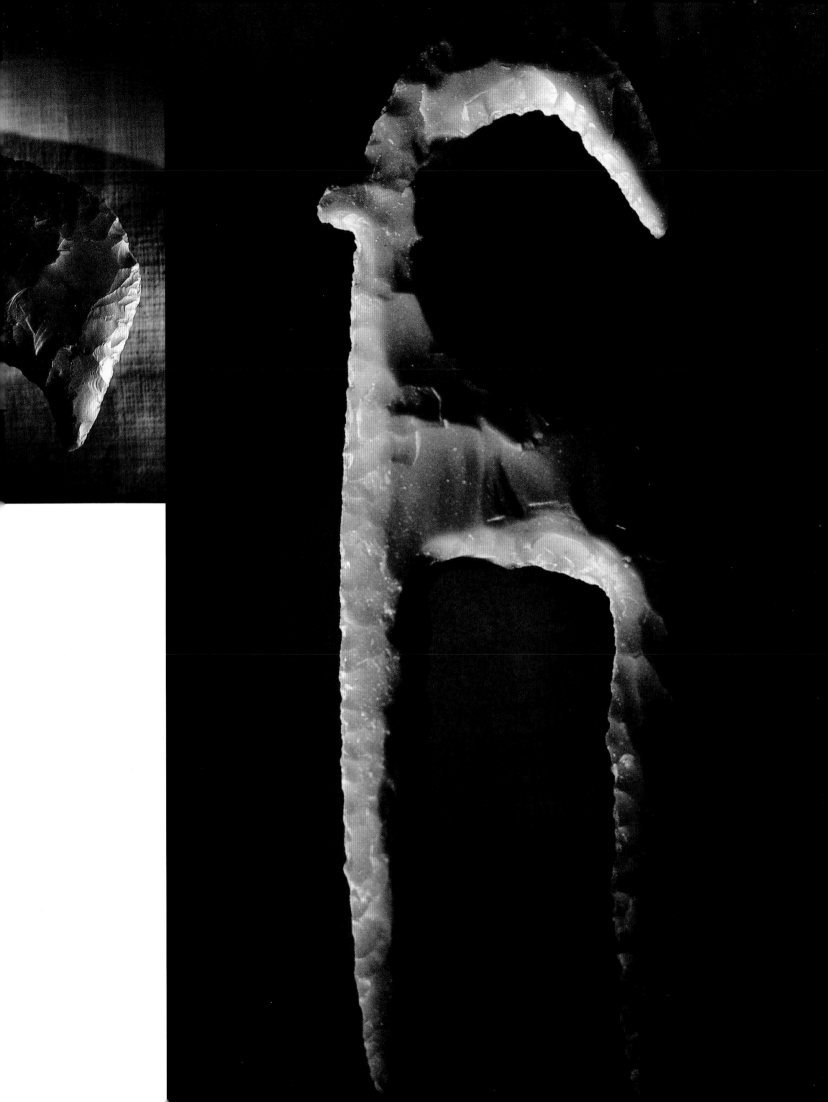

he site of a small fishing village called Raqote. He planned an enormous fortified city in a mix of Egyptian and Greek styles but did not live long enough to see it built. After he died in 323 B.C., his most trusted general, Ptolemy, took over Egypt and, in 305 B.C., had himself declared pharaoh of Egypt, founding a dynasty that ruled the country from Alexandria for almost three centuries. Ancient Alexandria was, by all accounts, a spectacular city. Accidental discoveries have been made in the seas off Alexandria for almost a century, but it is only recently that systematic exploration of the area has been carried out.

The earliest underwater discoveries were made by a French architect who found huge limestone blocks while extending the western port of the city. In 1933 a British pilot noticed a horseshoe shape under the water as he flew over the bay of Abuqir. Later work carried out at the order of Prince Omar Tosin resulted in the discovery of a large temple and a marble head of Alexander the Great. In the 1960s Egyptian diver Kamal Abu Sadaat noted many statues and blocks in his explorations. Much of the work being done now is based on his research.

Raising artifacts from underwater is an enormous technical feat, involving ropes, cranes, and careful engineering. Jean-Yves Empereur led the first scientific underwater excavations in 1995. He found 500 artifacts from the Ptolemaic period in the Qaitbay region, and his success led to formation of a Department of Underwater Archaeology within the SCA. The underwater exploration of this region has been carried out primarily by the French Institute under Empereur and by the European Institute under Franck Goddio.

The exquisite statue shown here dates to the Late Ptolemaic period and was found in the area of a temple of Isis. The style of clothing and the diadem with royal uraeus indicate that the statue represents a queen or goddess, probably Isis herself, wife of Osiris and an important deity throughout the pharaonic and Greco-Roman periods. She holds an ankh, the sign for life, in one hand, and her eyes were once inlaid. When discovered (with the aid of electronic sensing equipment) the sculpture was in four pieces, which were rejoined, carefully restored, and brought to Cairo for the Hidden Treasures exhibit.

GODDIO FOUND THIS STELA AT THE NOW UNDERWATER SITE OF Heraklion, where it had been brought by a Ptolemaic ruler to be reused as building stone. It dates to the reign of Nectanebo I of the 30th dynasty. On the top, the king makes offerings to the gods. Below this are 14 lines of text, which record a royal decree stating that a tenth of the taxes collected on imported goods should be donated to the temple of the goddess Neith in Sais.

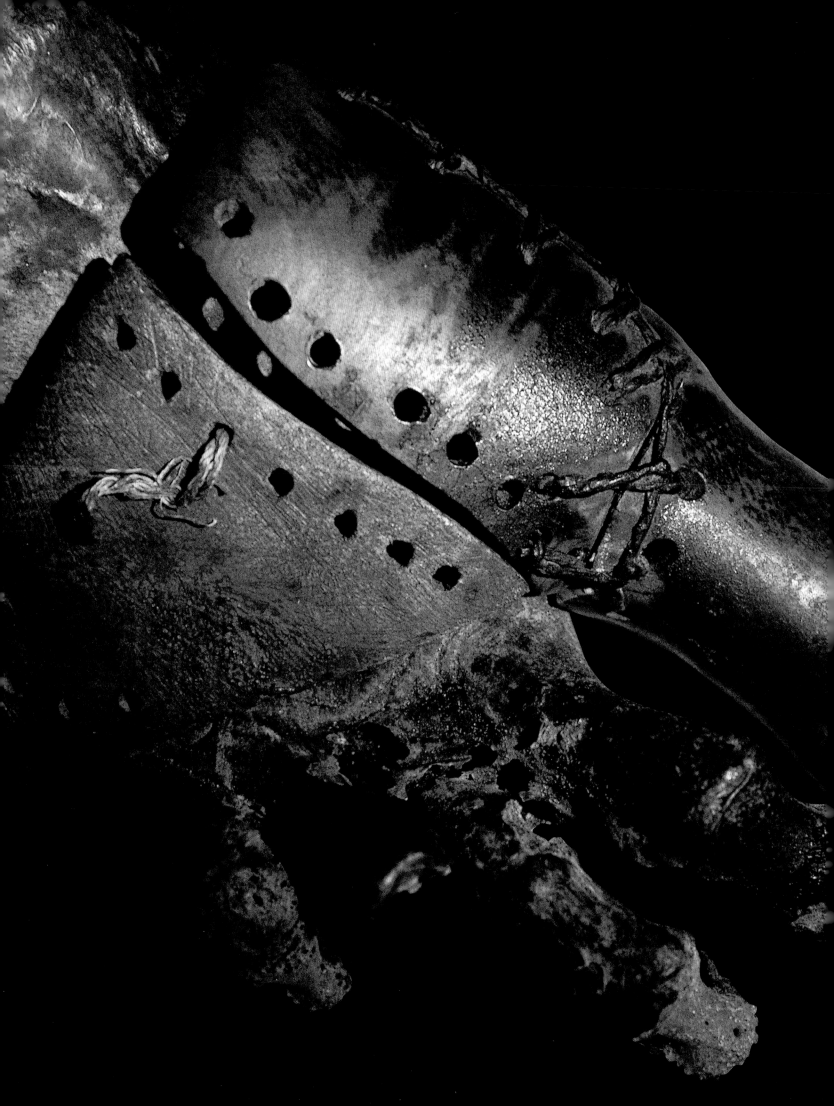

2000: Ancient False Toes

THIS WOODEN TOE, DATING TO THE THIRD INTERMEDIATE PERIOD, WAS found in December 2000 by a German team under Antonio Loprieno working in the Theban tomb of Meri, TT95. The original tomb dates to the New Kingdom but, like most of the other tombs in this area, was reused in later periods. This prosthetic toe is one of only three known examples, all from the Theban area and dating to the late New Kingdom or Third Intermediate period. The mummy to which it was attached was of a woman named Tabaketenmut, daughter of a priest named Bakamon. Tabaketenmut was between 50 and 60 years old when she died. She suffered from hardening of the arteries and may also have been diabetic. Paleopathological analysis shows that her right big toe had been amputated, and the condition of the artificial toe, whose bottom side shows signs of wear, tells us that she must have worn it during her lifetime. The workmanship of the prosthesis is excellent; it has been carved carefully to look as natural as possible. The manner in which it was set against the stump of her amputated big toe and attached with cords and a strap was skillful and effective.

PROSTHETIC TOE
Wood and leather
Total length of the prosthesis 12.3 cm;
   length of the toe 6.7 cm; maximum
   width of the prosthesis 8.0 cm;
   maximum height (when attached to
   the foot) 4.7 cm
Third Intermediate period, Dynasties 22
   to 23 (about 950–710 B.C.)
Thebes, intrusive shaft in the tomb of
   Meri, TT95
German excavation under Antonio
   Loprieno, 2000

HEADREST OF TETIANKHKEM;
OFFERING TABLET OF THE SEVEN SACRED OILS
Alabaster
Headrest: Disc diameter, 8 cm; Height of pillar 12.6 cm;
Diameter of pillar top 5.7 cm; Diameter of pillar base 7.6 cm
Tablet: Width 7.7 cm; Length 16.5 cm; Diameter 1.5 cm
Old Kingdom, Beginning of Dynasty 6
Saqqara, Teti pyramid complex
Excavations of Zahi Hawass, 2000

2000: The Teti Pyramid Complex

THESE EXQUISITE ARTIFACTS WERE FOUND DURING RECENT EXCAVATIONS near the pyramid of King Teti, first king of the 6th dynasty, who ruled from about 2345 B.C. to 2323 B.C. While my team was clearing the subsidiary complex of one of Teti's queens, a new tomb—a small, beautifully decorated mastaba—was found. The inscriptions on the walls of the chapel identified the tomb's owner as Tetiankh (also known as Tetiankhkem), the eldest son of Teti and therefore quite likely his crown prince. At the foot of the deep burial shaft was a sarcophagus of unpolished limestone whose lid had been slid open just far enough for a small child to slip through and steal the amulets and jewelry from the body. Inside the sarcophagus was the skeleton of a young man who died between the ages of 18 and 25. One historical source states that Teti was deposed and murdered in a palace coup; it is tempting to think that perhaps his crown prince was murdered at the same time, but there was not enough evidence left to determine whether Tetiankhkem had been killed or died a natural death.

Both the headrest and the offering tablet were found in the burial chamber. The headrest, which functioned as a sort of pillow for the mummy, stands on a base that was inscribed with the name and titles of the prince: "the Eldest Son of the King of his Body, the Sole Friend, Honored before the Great God, Tetiankh." The tablet is divided into seven sections, one for each of seven special oils, which would have been used to anoint the mummy before it was wrapped in linen, as well as in the rite of the Opening of the Mouth, a ceremony that served to revitalize the spirit of the deceased.

STANDING STATUE OF OFFICIAL
Wood
Height with base 62.4 cm
Old Kingdom, Dynasty 6
Saqqara, Teti pyramid complex
Excavations of Zahi Hawass, 1997

DURING OUR RECENT EXCAVATIONS IN THE COMPLEX OF TETI AT SAQQARA we found three beautiful wooden statues in the top layers of debris just south of the pyramid of Iput I, secondary wife of Teti and mother of Pepi I. None of the statues are inscribed, but they can be dated stylistically to the 6th dynasty. This statue shows an official holding a long staff, symbol of his office. The technique used here is interesting: The wood out of which the statue was carved was coated with mortar and then painted, giving the image a very lifelike appearance; the eyes are particularly striking. His wig was carved from a separate piece of wood, and—unusually for this period—the artist has added thick black wax, some of which has now fallen off, to deepen the modeling.

2001: An Ancient Doctor

beneath its sands. This fact is well known to modern tomb robbers, a group of whom were recently caught by the police in the vicinity of one of the Old Kingdom pyramids at the site. The area they were invading is relatively unexplored, so I decided to undertake some excavations near the tomb the thieves were attempting to rob and found a large cemetery dating to the 5th and 6th dynasties. Among the tombs was a square mastaba belonging to a royal physician of the late 5th dynasty (2494 B.C. to 2345 B.C.) or early 6th dynasty (2345 B.C. to 2181 B.C.) named Qar.

The tomb had been robbed in antiquity, but the ancient thieves left a number of artifacts behind. Among them was this offering table, which lists the various types of food and drink that were necessary for Qar's eternal survival in the afterlife, including bread of different sorts, beer, wine, milk, meat, fowl, and cult materials such as eye paint and incense. The tablet of the seven sacred oils is very similar to that of Tetiankhkem (page 198). The tools of Qar's trade—scalpels and other medical implements made of copper—were found in his burial chamber.

During excavations in the area of Qar's tomb, we found a cache of bronze statuettes that appear to have been buried during the 26th dynasty (664 B.C. to 525 B.C.). Among these was an image of Imhotep, the architect of the Step Pyramid at Djoser, which dominates the skyline of Saqqara. Imhotep was worshiped in the Late period as the god of medicine and conflated in the Ptolemaic period with Asklepios, Greek god of healing. Perhaps Qar, as a physician, was also associated with Imhotep.

OFFERING TABLE OF QAR
Alabaster
Diameter 31.5 cm; Height of base 7 cm
End of Dynasty 5 to early Dynasty 6
Saqqara
Excavations of Zahi Hawass, 2001

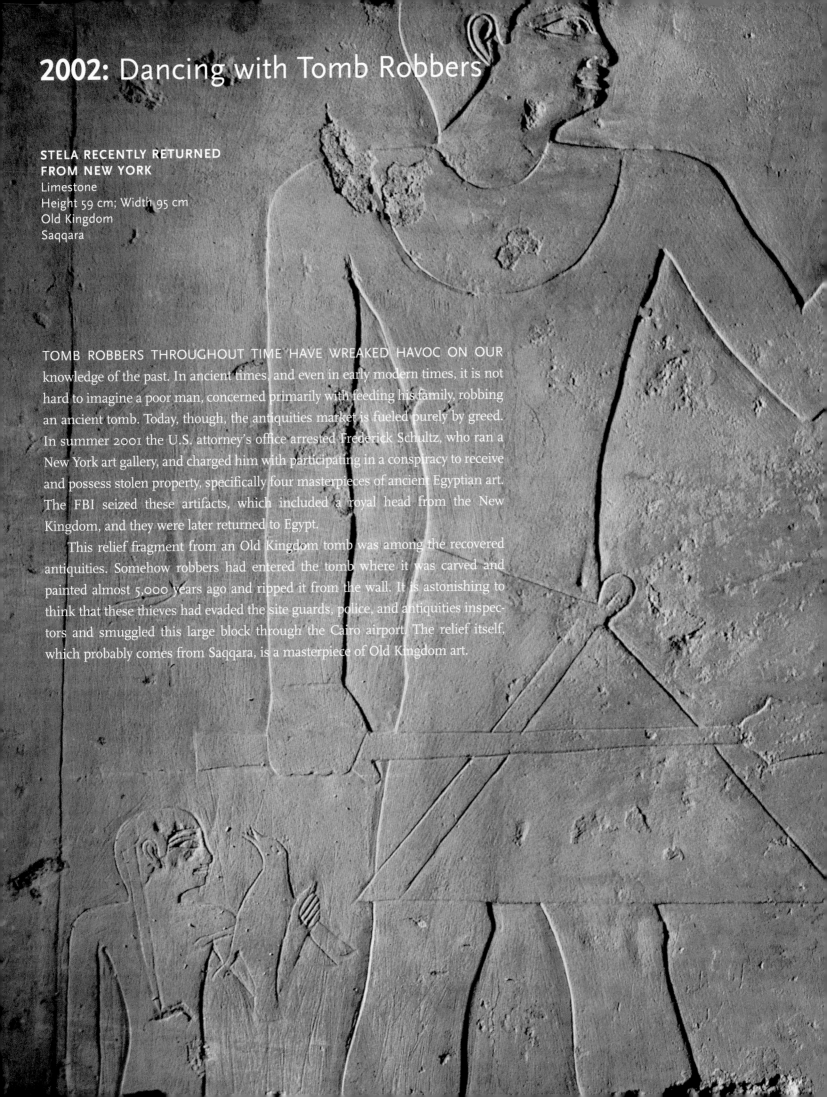

2002: Dancing with Tomb Robbers

**STELA RECENTLY RETURNED
FROM NEW YORK**
Limestone
Height 59 cm; Width 95 cm
Old Kingdom
Saqqara

TOMB ROBBERS THROUGHOUT TIME HAVE WREAKED HAVOC ON OUR knowledge of the past. In ancient times, and even in early modern times, it is not hard to imagine a poor man, concerned primarily with feeding his family, robbing an ancient tomb. Today, though, the antiquities market is fueled purely by greed. In summer 2001 the U.S. attorney's office arrested Frederick Schultz, who ran a New York art gallery, and charged him with participating in a conspiracy to receive and possess stolen property, specifically four masterpieces of ancient Egyptian art. The FBI seized these artifacts, which included a royal head from the New Kingdom, and they were later returned to Egypt.

This relief fragment from an Old Kingdom tomb was among the recovered antiquities. Somehow robbers had entered the tomb where it was carved and painted almost 5,000 years ago and ripped it from the wall. It is astonishing to think that these thieves had evaded the site guards, police, and antiquities inspectors and smuggled this large block through the Cairo airport. The relief itself, which probably comes from Saqqara, is a masterpiece of Old Kingdom art.

2002: Excavations at the Pyramid of Djedefre

CANOPIC JAR
Alabaster
Height 25 cm; Width 20 cm
Old Kingdom, Dynasty 4
Abu Rawash, queen's pyramid
of Djedefre
Swiss-Egyptian excavation, 2002

THE REMOTE SITE OF ABU RAWASH IS DOMINATED BY A ROCKY KNOLL ON which sits the remains of the pyramid of Khufu's son and successor, Djedefre, who had moved eight kilometers (five miles) to the north rather than staying at Giza, where his father had built what would remain the largest Egyptian pyramid. Djedefre ruled for only eight years and did not have time to finish his own monument.

In 1993 an Egyptian team from the Giza office began working at this site under my supervision. When the Supreme Council decided to give the concession to a Swiss-French team, I proposed that the Egyptian team continue to work at the site, creating a joint project.

Over the course of five years, the team, under the direction of Michel Valloggia, did excellent work. In 2002 the archaeologists found a small subsidiary pyramid near the main pyramid of Djedefre; this appears to have been built originally as a ritual pyramid, dedicated to the cult of the king himself. Many theories as to the purpose of these small pyramids have been proposed, from a burial place for the king's placenta or crowns to a structure associated with the king's Jubilee celebration (Sed festival). This pyramid, however, contained the burial of a queen. In the main chamber was a broken sarcophagus, a niche for canopic jars, this beautiful bowl, and many ceramic vessels, all very similar to the objects found in the tomb of Queen Hetepheres I.

Mummification was still in its infancy during the early part of the Old Kingdom. The removal of the viscera—lungs, intestines, liver, and stomach—to delay the process of decay was a new development, attested to for the first time during the reign of Khufu, in the burial of his mother, Hetepheres I. By the reign of Djedefre, as this new find shows, the four groups of viscera were placed into separate jars, which have acquired the misnomer of canopic jars. The current example represents the earliest type, simple in shape and with a plain stopper. In the Middle Kingdom human heads were added to these jars, and by the New Kingdom they could be surmounted by heads representing the four sons of Horus (pages 172–173).

The large bowl on the overleaf is inscribed with the two names of Djedefre's father, the Horus Medjedhu, King Khufu. It is an exquisite piece, large enough that it must be held with two hands, and translucent, the honey-colored alabaster glowing from within. Djedefre is known to have married at least two women, Hetepheres II and Khenetenkai. Whichever of these queens owned this tomb, she was most likely a daughter of Khufu himself and brought this bowl with her to Abu Rawash as a priceless treasure to take with her into the afterlife.

Diameter 52 cm
Old Kingdom, Dynasty 4
Abu Rawash, queen's pyramid of Djedefre
Swiss-Egyptian excavation, 2002

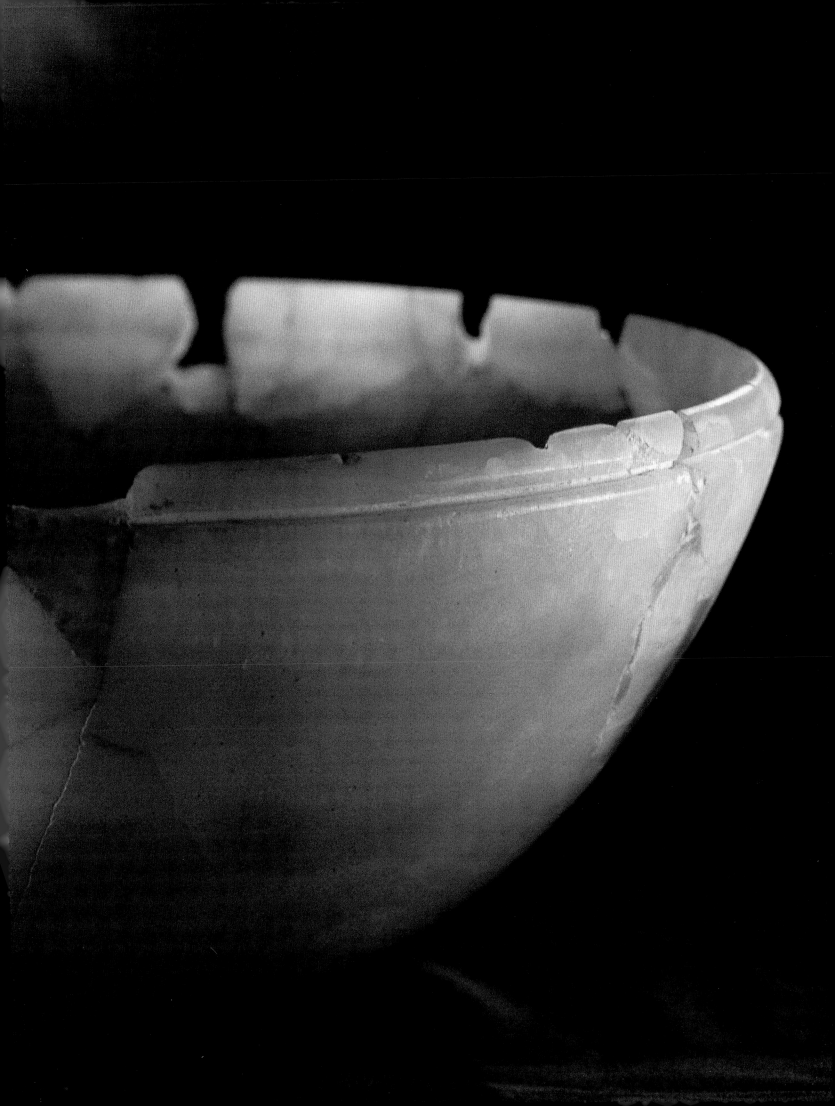

III. EXCITING NEW DISCOVERIES

FROM ASWAN TO SAQQARA

THE PAST TWO YEARS HAVE BEEN EXCITING ONES. THIS last section provides a brief glimpse at some of the work that is going on now in Egypt, at new secrets that are emerging from the sands. Our focus on conservation, preservation, and salvage archaeology continues to lead us to surprising new discoveries.

I. The Discovery of the Great Temple of Ramses II at Akhmim

The ancient city of Akhmim lies on the east bank of the Nile about 100 kilometers (60 miles) north of Luxor. The site has yielded remains dating back to the Predynastic period and continued to be occupied throughout pharaonic history. Akhmim was the capital of the ninth nome of Upper Egypt and the religious center of the fertility god Min, whose cult is attested as far back as the prehistoric period. Arab historians mention an enormous temple complex here, larger than Karnak. One of these writers reported that the sun had time to rise and then set again before he had finished exploring the ruins.

Akhmim was the center of Christianity in Upper Egypt, and a great church was built above the pharaonic temples; until recently, very little remained to be seen of the ancient remains. In September 1981 foundations were being dug for a new building when the ear and part of the wig of a colossal statue were discovered. The construction project was stopped and excavations carried out to uncover the rest of the statue, which was of Merytamun, wife and daughter of Ramses II. Part

of a Roman well was also found. Excavations continued in the area between 1981 and 1994 under the supervision of the Inspectorate of Sohag. The archaeologists discovered 70 percent of a large statue of Ramses II, about 13 meters (43 feet) high, broken into 16 pieces. This statue has not yet been restored. They also found the headless basalt statue of a priest named Khenty-Min dating from the 18th dynasty; a Roman statue, also headless, that may be of Venus; and a limestone statue of Amenhotep III that had been, like many older statues, usurped by Ramses II.

In 1991 the city council of Akhmim was constructing a post office about 45 meters (147 feet) to the north of the statue of Merytamun, near a modern cemetery. While trenches were being dug for the foundation of this building, under the careful supervision of the local inspectorate, the base of a large statue of Ramses II was uncovered. Unfortunately, excavations were limited by the presence of the modern cemetery, and the work had to be stopped. A wooden bridge was built over the remains of the

Base of a colossal statue of Ramses II

colossal statue so that the modern villagers could access the cemetery.

When I became head of the SCA, I spoke to Minister of Culture Farouk Hosni about Akhmim. He told me that President Mubarak had gone to visit the colossal statue of Merytamun and was very interested in the site. President Mubarak agreed to issue a decree ordering that the modern cemetery be moved to another location so that we could recommence the excavations.

I brought my team from Giza, led by archaeologist Mansour Boriak and epigrapher Noha Abdel Hafiz, to begin excavations; I go often to oversee the work. The base turned out to be part of a huge seated statue of Ramses II, the largest limestone statue of this king ever found. The head of the statue lay nearby, along with numerous stelae and parts of older royal statues that had been used by Ramses II as fill to level the area. The statue was originally about 13 meters (43 feet) high, and weighs more than 700 tons. We believe that it sat in front of the temple pylon (gateway). Christians had tried to destroy the statue when they built their church but succeeded only in damaging it. The lower part was too massive for them, so they ended up building a screen wall of baked brick to hide it from sight.

The statue represents Ramses II seated on a chair; behind his left leg stands Merytamun, and behind his right leg is his eldest daughter by Queen Isetnofret, Bint-anat. Ramses II married both of

Zahi Hawass at Akhmim with visiting dignitaries

these daughters, along with a third daughter, Nebitawy. These three women are buried in a tomb in the Valley of the Queens at Thebes. The king and his throne were both cut from a single block of limestone. The base is carved with scenes and inscriptions, including a scene showing the god Hapy holding the sign of unification and bound captives, each labeled with the name of a foreign country.

A local undertaker, realizing the potential of the area, decided to carry out his own excavations within the cemetery itself, with the collaboration of a member of the family that owned one of the tombs. Inside the burial chamber he found another colossal head of Ramses II, lying upside down beneath the level of the modern relics. The family tried to keep the find quiet, but rumors began to spread, and the police heard about it. They arrested the undertaker, who confessed. The tomb was placed under SCA supervision, and I was called in to examine the find. Inside the modern tomb, which was dark and smelled terrible, I found a huge head of Ramses II, 2.6 meters (9 feet) high, wearing the nemes headcloth.

I went recently to meet with the governor of Sohag to ask him to stop traffic from using the road that separates the recently discovered statue of Ramses II and the statue of Merytamun. We have now been able to dig some trenches and have determined that the courtyard of the great Temple of Min extends throughout this area. Very recently part of yet another colossal statue bearing the cartouches of Ramses II was discovered. We have sent five million pounds (810,000 dollars) to the Governorate of Sohag to fund the building of the new cemetery, after which we can start to move the old tombs to their new locations. We will continue to excavate in this area and uncover the great ancient temple to the god Min.

Noha Abdel Hafiz with a colossal head of Ramses II

Colossal statue of Merytamun

Torso of a Roman statue

Figure of Merytamun by the leg of her father

II. New Discoveries in the Quarry of the Unfinished Obelisk

The modern town of Aswan lies on the southernmost border of the ancient Egyptian state. The pharaonic settlement here lies both under the modern city and on the island of Elephantine, in the middle of the Nile. This frontier town was the gate for trade to the south, to the Nubian lands full of gold, ivory, and other exotic products. The tombs of the ancient governors of the area are carved into the western cliffs overlooking Elephantine; the biographical inscriptions contained within these tombs provide evidence of the importance of this area. Excavations carried out by the German Institute in Cairo on the island have added greatly to our understanding of the region.

In addition to the importance of this area as a border region and a trading center, Aswan was known for its quarries. The geologic character of the Nile Valley begins to change at Gebel el-Silsileh, north of Aswan. A vein of sandstone emerges from beneath the limestone that prevails to the north, the harder stone narrowing the floodplain. At Aswan, the underlying granite comes to the surface, creating the cataracts that mark the southern border of Egypt. The largest sandstone quarry in Egypt lies at Gebel el-Silsileh, where the stone for building the Theban temples was quarried. West of Aswan is an important quartzite quarry, and at Aswan itself are the granite quarries that provided casing material for Old Kingdom pyramids (one course at the pyramid of Khafre, and sixteen at the pyramid of Menkaure) and pyramid temples, and stone for statues and obelisks, many of which were set up in the New Kingdom temples at Luxor and Karnak.

There were four major granite quarries at Aswan. The one that concerns us here lies to the east of the Nile and has been nicknamed the Quarry of the Unfinished Obelisk because of the monumental obelisk that was carved into the bedrock and then abandoned because of a flaw in the stone. Egyptologists believe that this dates to the reign of Hatshepsut. This quarry has received a great deal of attention from scholars since the late 19th century. However, only recently have archaeologists begun to study the area and make careful records of what they see. The most important analysis before our current work was done by Dieter Arnold, who analyzed the techniques used by the ancients. He was able to show that the pharaonic quarrymen used diorite pounding balls to remove the stone surrounding the piece that was to be extracted, working downward from the surface and then undercutting the lower edge. It was not until Ptolemaic times that iron tools were used.

The site of the unfinished obelisk is very important and is a major tourist attraction. The SCA began studying the site in 1990, surveying the area. The survey was carried out at the east of the site, below an area of modern houses. The archaeologists have also cut excavation trenches and found important artifacts.

As part of the survey, the SCA team followed the outlines of the blocks that were cut in the

Graffiti of dophins, boats, and an obelisk in the unfinished obelisk quarry at Aswan

quarry. This was very difficult, as the quarry was used over an enormous span of time, from the Predynastic period into Roman times and even beyond. Cuttings made using different types of tools overlie one another, and it is very difficult to sort out traces of the many different types of objects cut from the stone: obelisks of various sizes, pillars, statues, offering tables, casing blocks, etc. The Ptolemaic and Roman quarrymen were able to use blocks left behind by the pharaonic workers because of mistakes or flaws in the stone, thus destroying much of the evidence left behind by the pharaohs.

When I became head of the SCA I began to oversee the work that was going on in the quarry. My teams have moved about 100,000 cubic meters of sand and granite rubble, and much new evidence of ancient quarrying activity has been uncovered and recorded. The beds of seven large obelisks were traced; the measurements of these can be compared with obelisks standing in Luxor or Karnak or, since many of these were taken during the early years of discovery, in Europe or America.

We also uncovered a huge block that looks as if it was planned as a colossal statue of Osiris. Near this statue was an inscription dating to year 25 of

Graffiti of ostriches represents the possibility of contact with the south.

the reign of Tuthmosis III, the 18th dynasty king who took the Egyptian empire to its greatest heights. This inscription tells us that the king ordered his architect to cut two obelisks for the temple of his father, Amon, at Karnak. The first of these obelisks is still standing; we now know that there was once a second.

Evidence for a harbor was also found in front of the quarry site. The cut stone would have been loaded onto boats here to be floated down the Nile to the sites where it would be used. A scene showing two huge obelisks being transported by Nile barge decorates the wall of the temple of Hatshepsut at Deir el-Bahri. The location of this quarry at the river's edge made the erection of such massive monolithic monuments possible. As further evidence for ancient stoneworking techniques, the team found thousands of diorite balls used as tools, mainly from the New Kingdom.

A great deal of graffiti, both inscriptional and pictorial, was recorded at the site. Pharaonic graffiti in red recording the lengths of a number of obelisks were noted; Greek comments were also found nearby. There was also an interesting group of inscriptions describing the different stages of work. Greek names were recorded by the SCA team, as well as Egyptian names written in Greek. Bes, god of pleasure and fun (page 147), was represented a number of times. He seems to have been a favorite god of the hardworking quarrymen. One unusual, well-executed drawing shows two obelisks: The larger is 171 centimeters (68 inches), the smaller 39.5 centimeters (15.8 inches). Another sketch shows a group of boats and dolphins drawn in black and red. The dolphins suggest that some of the workmen came from the north, from the delta or even from the Mediterranean. Contact with the south is represented by a troop of 12 ostriches of varying sizes.

STELA FROM THE QUARRY OF THE UNFINISHED OBELISK

QUARRY OF THE UNFINISHED OBELISK

III. Two Intact Tombs of Dynasty I at Saqqara

We have started a site management program at Saqqara to make sure that the riches of this important necropolis are preserved for future generations. There are many problems plaguing the site. For example, many of the antiquities found at the site were stored in 45 badly built magazines. The contents of these storerooms were poorly recorded, and the artifacts inside in danger from theives. Two new magazines have been built at the foot of the plateau, near the modern police station, and all of the objects have been moved into these buildings for conservation and recording. Conservation labs are being built to handle human remains and for restoration of artifacts; new offices for administration are also under way. Studies of the site are being carried out by an Italian and Egyptian team; these include careful documentation and publication of the 13 archaeological sites that constitute the larger site of Saqqara and new analyses of the risks that threaten the monuments.

The Early Dynastic tombs at Saqqara have been in need of restoration for many years. These are extremely important monuments, belonging to the most elite members of early Egyptian society. They are built of mud brick and have no limestone casing that might protect them from the elements. To preserve them properly we needed to excavate around their bases. I placed Mohamed Hagrass, whom I have made head of the new Department for the Study of the Pyramids, which I oversee, in charge of the day-to-day work and go twice a week to give the team direction. We began excavating south of the major tombs and discovered a large cemetery, in which we have found 22 tombs so far, all dating to the Predynastic and Early Dynastic periods. These do not look royal, but seem to be for important people. Each contains a false door built of mud brick. Above one of these, we found a slab of unshaped acacia, the local wood, on which is roughly drawn a man seated in front of an offering table. The hieroglyphic inscription cut onto this panel is not clear; not even the name is legible. Within the tombs, shafts sealed with mud brick contain bodies, all arranged in a fetal position. The pottery found associated with these bodies dates the burials to the Predynastic period, the 1st dynasty, and the 2nd dynasty.

Hagrass called me in great excitement this March to tell me that two of the burials were still intact. After a night in which I could barely sleep, dreaming of the history that we might uncover the next day, I drove out to Saqqara to examine the new finds. The first tomb lies about three meters (ten feet) underground. When we first explored this shaft, it was sealed with mud brick, the spaces between the bricks filled with mortar. I removed several blocks from the top to allow the stale, possibly harmful air within the chamber to disperse. The next day we removed the rest of the blocking. I then entered the tomb and found a skeleton curled in the fetal position, covered in linen with only the head showing. There were no other artifacts.

Wooden panel of acacia

I asked Saleh Bedair, former dean of the Faculty of Medicine at Cairo University and one of the consultants to the SCA for the study of human remains, to come and work with us. His analysis of the skeleton revealed that it was a woman who died at the age of about 35. Her skull had been broken and there were traces of blood on one of her legs. This evidence suggests that she was murdered. It has long been believed that royal retainers were sacrificed during the 1st dynasty; the new discovery provides support for this theory and evidence that ritual sacrifice was also practiced at Saqqara, information that may force us to reexamine our attribution of these tombs to non-royal officials. Perhaps queens were buried in some of the monumental tombs and were sent into the afterlife accompanied by the women who had served them during life.

The second intact tomb may be even more interesting than the first. About 5 meters (17 feet) underground, blocked by a mud-brick wall, was a wooden coffin, which appears to be made of cedarwood from Lebanon. This was an expensive material, and indicates that the person was very important. The burial shaft was very small, and the coffin barely fit inside. The ceiling of the chamber just cleared the lid of the sarcophagus, so I called for Ahmed and Talal el-Kirity to help move it safely. We prepared the coffin carefully, tying the lid with ropes, and moved it slowly and gently. It took about seven hours to move it out of its chamber. We then took it to the lab and found that the lid was sealed. Inside, in the fetal position, was a skeleton on whose legs were the remains of resins. This is the earliest indication we have found to date of mummification in Egypt.

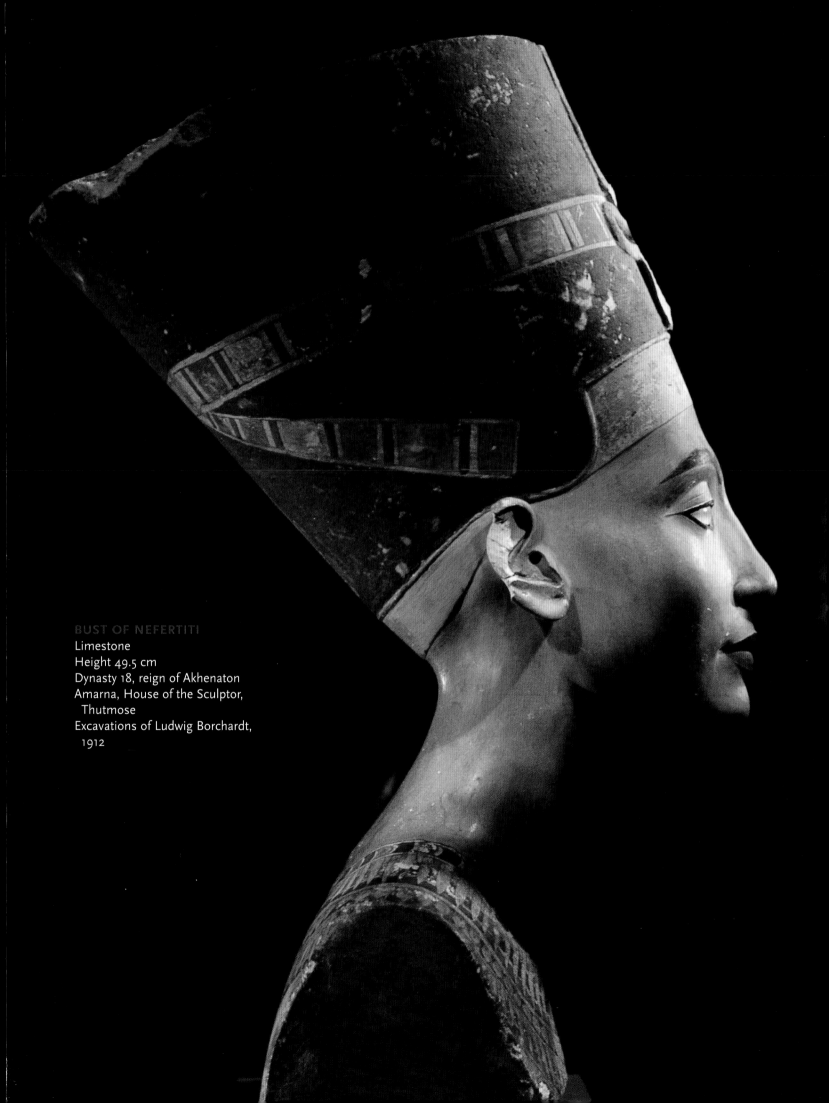

BUST OF NEFERTITI
Limestone
Height 49.5 cm
Dynasty 18, reign of Akhenaton
Amarna, House of the Sculptor,
  Thutmose
Excavations of Ludwig Borchardt,
  1912

The Lost Queen

This masterpiece of ancient sculpture is the only object in the book that is not in the Cairo Museum. It was found by Ludwig Borchardt at Tell el-Amarna, in the house of a master sculptor named Thutmose, and depicts Queen Nefertiti, wife of Akhenaton in the tall blue crown of Tefnut. The loss of this portrait head, after the mask of Tutankhamun the most famous work of art from ancient Egypt, is still a point of contention with Egyptian Egyptologists, and with the many foreign archaeologists who support us.

The German excavations of the pre–World War I seasons were subject to an equitable division of finds: Half went to the country, organization, or individual who funded the work, and the other half stayed in Egypt. At the end of each season, the Egyptian Antiquities Service and the foreign mission hammered out the details of the division. At the end of the 1912 season during which this head was found, the Egyptian officials in charge of the division let the head go to Germany. Many people, myself included, believe that Borchardt disguised the head by encasing it in mud plaster so that the Egyptians, believing it to be relatively unimportant, would let it leave the country.

When the newly cleaned and restored head was put on display at the Berlin Museum several years later, the Egyptian Antiquities Service requested its return. An agreement between Egyptian and German officials was reached just before the Second World War, and Nefertiti was prepared for her return. However, before she left, Hitler came to see her for the first time, and refused to let her leave.

In the early 1990s, it was first proposed that one of the three mummies found in a side chamber of the tomb of Amenhotep II is Nefertiti. These bodies have been studied scientifically several times, first in 1912 by Elliot Smith, and again in 1980 by James Harris and Edward Wente. One of these mummies is of an older woman who is tentatively identified as queen Tiye, wife of Amenhotep III and mother of Akhenaton. The second body is of a young boy. The idea that the third mummy is Nefertiti's has recently been revived in a television program. In reality, even the gender of this mummy is still in question, and a number of points, including its age, which is significantly younger than Nefertiti should have been at death, argue against this identification.

Many people would love to see this debate resolved through the use of DNA analysis. However, a certain uninterrupted length of the DNA chain must be recovered for accurate analysis to be carried out. Much of the DNA within mummies has decayed, and sufficiently long sequences have not yet been able to be recovered. The few positive results gained using current techniques are in each case likely to be the result of modern contamination. In fact, the SCA did do a chromosome test on this mummy, and determined that it was male. However, we consider this result tentative, and leave open the possibility that it is a product of contamination.

The available technology for DNA analysis is not yet reliable, and there are no labs in Egypt capable of doing "ancient DNA" research. Once labs have developed effective methods for analyzing shorter sequences of DNA, we will allow them to be used on Egyptian mummies. Perhaps many mysteries will finally be solved!

Final Note

We are entering an exciting era in Egyptian archaeology. I am the first of a new generation of Egyptian Egyptologists to hold the chair of the Supreme Council of Antiquities, and I am using my position to bring archaeology in Egypt into the 21st century. My primary focus will continue to be on conservation and preservation. If we simply continue to uncover new material without treating what has already been discovered properly, everything will disappear. Endangered sites, such as those in the delta, must be given priority. I have stopped all new excavations in Upper Egypt; only long-term projects or missions focused on conservation and recording will be allowed to work from Cairo to Aswan. Excavation in the delta is welcome and encouraged, as these sites are under great threat from the rising water table; the growing population, with its increased needs for housing and infrastructure; and modern agricultural techniques, whose methods damage the ancient sites.

Foreign missions are and will continue to be important contributors to our work. Expeditions from America, Germany, France, Italy, Austria, Spain, Poland, the Czech Republic, Britain, and Japan are working to conserve our past. Some of these missions are working in the delta and the desert, and others are in Upper Egypt, either continuing with projects that were begun long ago or doing important epigraphic and conservation work. Many missions work in the Theban area, recording tombs on the west bank or working in the temples of Luxor and Karnak. The water table here, as in most of Egypt, is dangerously high and overloaded with salt, threatening the antiquities. The problem in Luxor has been studied by a Swedish company, and construction of a new sewage system will begin under a grant from the U.S. Agency for International Development.

I do not allow untrained amateurs to work in Egypt. So far this year, the permanent committee of the SCA has turned down 13 applications because the projects were not professional and threatened to damage rather than illuminate our ancient past. This makes some people angry, but the monuments must come first.

Most important to me for the future of Egyptian archaeology is that our native scholars are trained properly. I have sent a number of my best inspectors to graduate school. These young Egyptians have made me a pledge: When they return with their doctorates, they will continue to work with the SCA, helping me to build it into a model for the future.

I am also making sure that Egyptian inspectors are being trained in the most modern methods of excavation. There is currently a field school at Memphis and in the Fayum run by the American Research Center in Egypt, and another in the Sinai run by the SCA, where young archaeologists are being trained in modern techniques. Many Egyptian archaeologists, including Ali Radwan, Adel Hakim Karara, and Mansour Boriak, are teaching in foreign and Egyptian field schools. Karara is now working with me in the tombs of the 26th dynasty Sheikh Soby, where we will soon open three new, intact tombs belonging to the members of the Djed-Khonsu-iufankh family. Boriak is supervising the excavations at Akhmim, and I will continue working at Akhmim and Saqqara as well as Giza.

Before we end, I want to tell you one more story, about a secret that still lies hidden from modern eyes. This was revealed to me by Sheikh Ali, the member of the Abd el-Rassoul family that I met as a young man while working on the west bank of Thebes. One night, as we drank tea together, he said to me, "I will tell you a secret. I can tell that you are the only one who can discover the hidden chamber inside the tomb of Seti I." He continued, "I am a man who can foretell certain things, and I can see that, though you are young now, one day you will become a famous archaeologist and you will fulfill the dreams of our family. If you come with me tomorrow, I will show you."

He took me to the tomb of Seti I, the father of Ramses the Great. We entered the burial chamber and he said, "Look, there is the beginning of a tunnel which goes back about 100 meters [330 feet]. At the end you will find the true burial chamber of Seti." I asked how he knew this, and he told me: "Many members of my family were working with Carter at the Tomb of Tutankhamun, including myself, although I was only a young boy. Carter used the tomb of Seti I as a storage and conservation room for the artifacts that came from the tomb of King Tut. My cousins and I stayed in the tomb of Seti for long periods of time while this work was going on, and we

explored every inch of it. We know that there is a hidden chamber inside the tomb that has not yet been discovered." Sheikh Ali never lost hope of finding it, but was never able to get permission to continue his search. Since he was not a scholar, although the tunnel itself was relatively common knowledge, his ideas were dismissed as hearsay and legend.

But I thought to myself that there might be some truth behind his theories. After all, his family had been instrumental in most of the great discoveries made in the Valley of the Kings in modern times. In July 2003 I went to the tomb of Seti I to restore four pieces of relief that have recently been returned to Egypt by the Michael C. Carlos Museum in Atlanta, through the good offices of Bonnie Speed, director of the museum, and Peter Lacovara, senior Egyptologist there.

While I was there, I decided to try to explore the tunnel. I entered the darkness of the sloping passageway first, armed only with a flashlight. Stone rubble fell around us, and I had to put my hand on top of my head to protect myself. But after 66 meters (217 feet) we could go no farther and were forced to turn back. This winter we will make a serious exploration of this tunnel. It may be that the sheikh was right. No artifacts were ever found inside Seti I's tomb (although his mummy was in the Deir el-Bahri cache), so perhaps his true burial chamber lies at the end of this tunnel. We will soon build arches to make this fascinating passage into the past safe to travel, and then we will see what lies beyond.

The adventure will continue.

Zahi Hawass examining the skeleton found recently in an Early Dynasty burial at Saqqara

Timeline of Ancient Egypt

Late Predynastic (circa 3100 B.C.)	Early Dynastic (ca 2950-2575 B.C.)	Old Kingdom (ca 2575-2150 B.C.)	First Intermediate Period (ca 2125-1975 B.C.)	Middle Kingdom (ca 1975-1640 B.C.)	Second Intermediate Period (ca 1630-1520 B.C.)
3000 B.C.		2500		2000	1500

o dynasty	1st dynasty	4th dynasty	9th-10th dynasties	11th dynasty	14th dynasty
Ka	Aha (Menes)	Snefru	Meryibre	Mentuhotep II	Nehesy
Ro	Djer	Khufu	Khety	(Nebhepetre)	
Narmer	Djet	Redjedef	Merikare	Mentuhotep III	15th dynasty
	Den	Khafre	Ity	Mentuhotep IV	HYKSOS
	Anedjib	Nebka II			Sheshi
	Semerkhet	Menkaure	11th dynasty	12th dynasty	Khyan
	Qa'a	Shepseskaf	Mentuhotep I	Amenemhet I	Apepi
			Inyotef I	Senusret I	Khamudi
	2nd dynasty	5th dynasty	Inyotef II	Amenemhet II	
	Hotepsekhemwy	Userkaf	Inyotef III	Senusret II	16th-17th dynasties
	Reneb	Sahure		Senusret III	Inyotef V
	Nynetjer	Neferirkare		Amenemhet III	Sebekemzaf I
	Peribsen	Shepseskare		Amenemhet IV	Nebireyeraw
	Sekhemib	Neferefre		Queen Sobeknefru	Sebekamzaf II
	Khasekhemwy	Neuserre			Ta'o I
		Menkauhor		13th dynasty	Ta'o II
	3rd dynasty	Djedkare		Wegaf	Kamose
	Djoser	Unas		Amenemhet V	
	Nebka I			Harnedjheriotef	
	Khaba	6th dynasty		Amenyqemau	
	Huni	Teti		Sebekhotep I	
		Userkare		Hor	
		Pepi I		Amenemhet VII	
		Merenre I		Sebekhotep II	
		Pepi II		Khendjer	
		Merenre II		Sebekhotep III	
				Neferhotep I	
		7th-8th dynasties		Sebekhotep IV	
		Qakare (Iby)		Sebekhotep V	
		Neferkaure		Aye	
		Neferkauhor		Mentuemzaf	
		Neferirkare II		Dedumose II	
				Neferhotep III	

Key

Ramses II Principal ruler

PERSIAN Foreign or immigrant ruler of Egypt

New Kingdom (ca 1539-1075 B.C.)	Third Intermediate Period (ca 1075-715 B.C.)	Late Period (ca 715-332 B.C.)	Greco-Roman Period (332 B.C.-A.D. 395)	Roman conquest (30 B.C.)

1000		500		A.D. 1

New Kingdom	Third Intermediate Period	Late Period	Greco-Roman Period
18th dynasty	**21st dynasty**	**25th dynasty NUBIAN**	**Macedonian dynasty**
Ahmose	Smendes I	Shabaka	Alexander the Great
Amenhotep I	Amenemnisu	Shebitku	
Thutmose I	Psusennes I	Taharqa	**Ptolemaic dynasty**
Thutmose II	Amenemope	Tantamani	Ptolemy I-X
Queen Hatshepsut	Osorkon I		Cleopatra Berenice
Thutmose III	Siamun	**26th dynasty**	Ptolemy XI-XII
Amenhotep II	Psusennes II	Psamtek I	Cleopatra VII
Thutmose IV		Necho II	
Amenhotep III	**High Priests**	Psamtek II	
Akhenaten	Herihor	Apries	
(Amenhotep IV)	Piankh	Amasis	
Smenkhkare	Pinedjem I	Psamtek III	
Queen Ankhetkheprure	Masaherta		
Tutankhamun	Menkheperre	**27th dynasty PERSIAN**	
Aye	Smendes II	Cambyses	
Horemheb	Pinedjem II	Darius I	
	Psusennes III	Xerxes	
19th dynasty		Artaxerxes I	
Ramses I	**22nd dynasty**	Darius II	
Seti I	Shoshenq I		
Ramses II	Osorkon II	**28th dynasty (Persians expelled)**	
Merneptah	Takelot I	Amyrtaeus	
Seti II	Shoshenq II		
Amenmesse	Osorkon III	**29th dynasty**	
Siptah	Takelot II	Nepherites I	
Queen Tawosret	Shoshenq III	Psammuthis	
	Pami	Hakor	
20th dynasty	Shoshenq V	Nepherites II	
Sethnakhte	Osorkon V		
Ramses III	Harsiese	**30th dynasty**	
Ramses IV		Nectanebo I	
Ramses V	**23rd dynasty**	Djedhor	
Ramses VI	Pedibastet	Nectanebo II	
Ramses VII	Shoshenq IV		
Ramses VIII	Osorkon IV	**31st dynasty PERSIAN**	
Ramses IX	Takelot III	Artaxerxes III	
Ramses X	Rudamon	Arses	
Ramses XI	Iuput	Darius III	
	Nimlot		
	Peftjauawybast		
	24th dynasty		
	Tefnakhte		
	Bakenrenef		
	25th dynasty NUBIAN		
	Kashta		
	Piye		

Index

Zahi Hawass
Photographs by Kenneth Garrett

Published by the National Geographic Society

John M. Fahey, Jr., *President and Chief Executive Officer*

Gilbert M. Grosvenor, *Chairman of the Board*

Nina D. Hoffman, *Executive Vice President*

Prepared by the Book Division

Kevin Mulroy, *Vice President and Editor-in-Chief*

Charles Kogod, *Illustrations Director*

Marianne R. Koszorus, *Design Director*

Staff for this Book

Lisa Lytton, *Editor*

Janice Kamrin, *Text Editor*

Judy Klein, *Contributing Editor*

Rebecca Lescaze, *Contributing Editor*

Jane Menyawi, *Illustrations Editor*

Lisa Lytton, *Art Director*

Carl Mehler, *Director of Maps*

Gary Colbert, *Production Director*

Lewis Bassford, *Production Project Manager*

Meredith Wilcox, *Illustrations Assistant*

Alexandra Littlehales, *Design Assistant*

Manufacturing and Quality Control

Christopher A. Liedel, *Chief Financial Officer*

Phillip L. Schlosser, *Managing Director*

John T. Dunn, *Technical Director*

Vincent P. Ryan, *Manager*

Clifton M. Brown, *Manager*

One of the world's largest nonprofit scientific and educational organizations, the National Geographic Society was founded in 1888 "for the increase and diffusion of geographic knowledge." Fulfilling this mission, the Society educates and inspires millions every day through its magazines, books, television programs, videos, maps and atlases, research grants, the National Geographic Bee, teacher workshops, and innovative classroom materials. The Society is supported through membership dues, charitable gifts, and income from the sale of its educational products. This support is vital to National Geographic's mission to increase global understanding and promote conservation of our planet through exploration, research, and education.

For more information, please call 1-800-NGS LINE (647-5463) or write to the following address:
National Geographic Society
1145 17th Street N.W.
Washington, D.C. 20036-4688 U.S.A.

Visit the Society's Web site at www.nationalgeographic.com.

Published by the National Geographic Society, 1145 17th Street N.W., Washington, D.C. 20036

Library of Congress Cataloging-in-Publication Data available upon request.

ISBN 0-7922-6319-7

ILLUSTRATION CREDITS:
Page 13: National Geographic Maps
Pages 21, 108, 109: Zahi Hawass Collection
Page 22: From 'Album du Musee de Boulaq,' 1871
Pages 25, 27,107, 111: Saqqara Archives

Printed in Italy